NPCA National Park Guide Series

NATIONAL PARKS
AND CONSERVATION ASSOCIATION

GUIDE TO NATIONAL PARKS
HEARTLAND REGION

Written and compiled by Russell D. Butcher for the National Parks and
Conservation Association and edited by Lynn P. Whitaker.

NPCA is America's only private, nonprofit citizen organization dedicated solely
to protecting, preserving, and enhancing the U.S. National Park System. The
association's mission is to protect and enhance America's National Park System
for present and future generations.

Guilford, Connecticut

Photo credits: pages i, iii, 8-9, 29 © Carr Clifton; pages iv-v, 79 © Willard Clay; pages 1, 50-51 © Fred Hirschmann; pages 4-5, 66-67 © Laurence Parent; pages 11, 26-27, 71, 95 © John Elk III; pages 15, 37, 42 © Craig Blacklock/Larry Ulrich Stock; pages 21, 53 © Larry Ulrich; pages 31, 73, 89 © David Muench; page 45 © Jeff Foott; page 55 © Les Blacklock/Larry Ulrich Stock; pages 61, 63, 84-85 © Tom Till.

Maps: © Trails Illustrated, a division of National Geographic Maps
Cover and text design: Adam Schwartzman
Cover photo: Badlands, Theodore Roosevelt National Park, North Dakota (© Carr Clifton)

Library of Congress Cataloging-in-Publication Data

Butcher, Russell D.
      National Parks and Conservation Association guide to national parks: heartland region / written and compiled by Russell D. Butcher for the National Parks and Conservation Association : and edited by Lynn P. Whitaker.
      — 1st ed.
          p. cm. — (NPCA national park guide series)
      ISBN 0-7627-0571-X
      1. National parks and preserves—Middle West Guidebooks. 2. Middle West Guidebooks. I. Whitaker, Lynn P. II. Title. III. Series.
      F350.3.B88   1999
      917.704'33—dc21   99-23821
                                                                                        CIP

♻ Printed on recycled paper
Printed and bound in Quebec, Canada
First edition/First printing

National Parks
and Conservation Association

Thomas C. Kiernan
President

Dear Reader:

Welcome to the National Parks and Conservation Association's national park guidebooks—a series designed to help you to discover America's most significant scenery, history, and culture found in the more than 370 areas that make up the U.S. National Park System.

The park system represents the best America has to offer for our natural, historical, and cultural heritage—a collection of resources that we have promised to preserve "unimpaired" for future generations. We hope that, in addition to giving you practical information to help you plan your visits to national park areas, these guides also will help you be a more aware, more responsible visitor to our parks. The cautions offered at the beginning of these guides are not to frighten you away but to remind you that we all have a role in protecting the parks. For it is only if each and every one of us takes responsibility that these special places will be preserved and available for future generations to enjoy.

For more than three-quarters of a century, the National Parks and Conservation Association has been America's leading citizen advocacy group working solely to protect the national parks. Whether fighting to preserve the wilderness character of Cumberland Island National Seashore, preventing the expansion of a major airport outside the Everglades, stopping a coal mine at Cumberland Gap, or defeating legislation that could lead to the closure of many national parks, NPCA has made the voices of its members and supporters heard in efforts to protect the resources of our national parks from harm.

We hope that you will join in our commitment. Remember: when you visit the parks, take only pictures, and leave only footprints.

1776 Massachusetts Avenue, N.W., Washington, D.C. 20036-1904
Telephone (202) 223-NPCA(6722) • Fax (202) 659-0650

♻ PRINTED ON RECYCLED PAPER

CONTENTS

1
11
15
21
31
37
45
55
63
71

Heartland Region

NORTH DAKOTA

Fort Union Trading Post NHS

Lake Sakakawea

Theodore Roosevelt NP North Unit

Knife River Indian Villages NHS

Theodore Roosevelt NP South Unit

Lake Oahe

Bismark

Fargo

Voyageurs NP

Grand P

MINNESOTA

Duluth

St. C

SOUTH DAKOTA

Jewel Cave NM

Mount Rushmore N MEM

Pierre

Lake Sharpe

Minneapolis

St. Paul

Mississippi NRRA

Pipestone NM

Badlands NP

Wind Cave NP

Lake Francis Case

Sioux Falls

Effigy Mou

Niobrara NSR

Missouri NRR

IOWA

Agate Fossil Beds NM

Scotts Bluff NM

Herbert Hoover

Des Moines

Io

NEBRASKA

Platte

Omaha

Homestead NM of America

Lincoln

MISSO

Nicodemus NHS

Brown vs. Board of Education NHS

Kansas City

Fort Larned NHS

Salina

Tallgrass Prairie N PRES

Topeka

Harry S Truman NHS

Jefferso

Great Bend

Fort Scott

Arkansas

Wichita

Fort Scott NHS

Springfield

KANSAS

George Washington Carver NM

Wilso

| 0 | 100 | 200 | Miles |
| 0 | 100 | 200 | 300 | Kilometers |

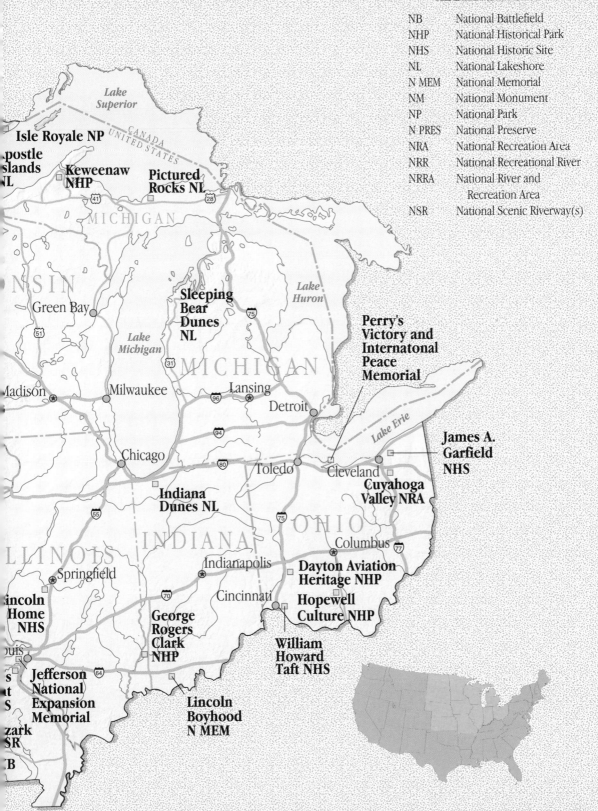

ABBREVIATIONS

NB — National Battlefield
NHP — National Historical Park
NHS — National Historic Site
NL — National Lakeshore
N MEM — National Memorial
NM — National Monument
NP — National Park
N PRES — National Preserve
NRA — National Recreation Area
NRR — National Recreational River
NRRA — National River and
  Recreation Area
NSR — National Scenic Riverway(s)

Lake Superior

Isle Royale NP

-postle slands NL

Keweenaw NHP

Pictured Rocks NL

CANADA
UNITED STATES

MICHIGAN

-NSIN

Green Bay

Lake Michigan

Sleeping Bear Dunes NL

Lake Huron

MICHIGAN

Perry's Victory and Internatonal Peace Memorial

Madison

Milwaukee

Lansing

Detroit

Chicago

Lake Erie

Toledo

Cleveland

James A. Garfield NHS

Cuyahoga Valley NRA

Indiana Dunes NL

OHIO

INDIANA

Columbus

-LLINOIS

Springfield

Indianapolis

Dayton Aviation Heritage NHP

-incoln Home NHS

Cincinnati

Hopewell Culture NHP

-uis

George Rogers Clark NHP

William Howard Taft NHS

Jefferson National Expansion Memorial

Lincoln Boyhood N MEM

-zark SR

B

NATIONAL GEOGRAPHIC MAPS
TRAILS ILLUSTRATED
©1999 Trails Illustrated, a division of National Geographic Maps

▲ *Squaw Bay Caves, Apostle Islands National Lakeshore, Wisconsin*

General Information

Whether you're an American history buff or a birdwatcher, a lover of rocky coastlines or marshy swamps, a dedicated environmentalist or a weekend rambler, and whether you're seeking a way to spend a carefully planned month-long vacation or an unexpectedly free sunny afternoon—the national parks are for you. They offer a broad spectrum of natural and cultural resources in all 50 states as well as Guam, Puerto Rico, the Virgin Islands, and American Samoa where you can learn, exercise, participate in activities, and be constantly moved and inspired by the riches available. Perhaps most important of all, as one of the National Park System's 280 million annual visitors, you become part of the attempt to preserve our natural and historical treasures for present and future generations.

This guidebook will help you do that, as one in a series of eight Regional National Park Guides covering all the units in the National Park System. This section of general information provides both an overview of key facts that can be applied to every unit and a brief history of the National Parks and Conservation Association (NPCA).

SPECIAL PARK PASSES

Some parks charge entrance fees to help offset their operational costs. Several options for special entrance passes are available, enabling you to choose the most appropriate and economical way for you and your family and friends to visit sites.

Park Pass: For this annual entrance permit to a specific fee-charging park, monument, historic site, or recreation area in the National Park System, the cost is usually $10 or $15 depending on the area. Such a pass does not cover any fees other than entrance for permit holder and any accompanying passengers in a private noncommercial vehicle or, in the case of walk-in facilities, the permit holder's spouse, children, and parents. The pass may be purchased in person or by mail from the unit at which it will be used. It is nontransferable and nonrefundable.

Golden Eagle Passport: This annual entrance pass admits visitors to all the federal lands that charge entrance fees; these include national parks, monuments, historic sites, recreation areas, national forests, and national wildlife refuges. The pass costs $50 and is valid for one year from purchase. It does not cover any fees other than entrance for permit holder and any accompanying passengers in a private noncommercial vehicle or, in the case of walk-in facilities, the holder's spouse, children, and parents. The Golden Eagle Passport may be purchased in person or by mail from the National Park Service, Office of Public Inquiries, Room 1013, U.S. Department of the Interior, 18th & C Streets, N.W., Washington, DC 20240 (202-208-4747) or at any of the seven National Park Service field offices, any of the nine U.S. Forest Service regional offices, or any national park unit and other federal areas that charge an entrance fee. It is nontransferable and nonrefundable.

Golden Age Passport: A one-time $10 fee for this pass allows lifetime entrance to all federal fee-charging areas as described in the Golden Eagle Passport section for citizens and permanent residents of the United States who are 62 years of age or older and any accompanying passengers in a private noncommercial vehicle or, in the case of walk-in facilities, the holder's spouse and children. This pass also entitles the holder to a 50 percent discount on use fees charged in park areas. The Golden Age Passport must be obtained IN PERSON at any of the locations listed in the Golden Eagle Passport section; mail requests are not accepted. Applicants must provide proof of age, such as a driver's license or birth certificate, or sign an affidavit attesting to eligibility.

Golden Access Passport: This free lifetime entrance permit to all federal fee-charging areas as described in the Golden Eagle Passport section is available for citizens and permanent residents of the United States who are visually impaired or permanently disabled and any accompanying passengers in a private noncommercial vehicle or, in the case of walk-in facilities, the permit holder's spouse, children, and parents. It also entitles the holder to a 50 percent discount on use fees charged in park areas. The Golden Access Passport must be obtained IN PERSON at any of the locations listed in the Golden Eagle Passport section; mail requests are not accepted. Applicant must provide proof of eligibility to receive federal benefits or sign an affidavit attesting to one's eligibility.

PASSPORT TO YOUR NATIONAL PARKS

The *Passport to Your National Parks* is a special commemorative item designed to serve as a companion for park visitors. This informative and unique publication records each visit through special regional and national stamps and cancellations. When you visit any national park, be sure to have your Passport canceled with a rubber stamp marking the name of the park and the date you were there. The Passport gives you the opportunity to share and relive your journey through America's national parks and will become a travel record to cherish for years. Passports cost $4.95; a full set of ten national and regional stamps is $3.95. The national parks represented in the stamp set vary from year to year. For ordering information, call 800-821-2903, or write to Eastern National Park & Monument Association, 110 Hector Street, Suite 105, Conshohocken, PA 19428.

HELPFUL TRIP-PLANNING PUBLICATIONS

Two volumes offer descriptive text on the National Park System: *Exploring Our National Parks and Monuments,* by Devereux Butcher (ninth edition by Russell D. Butcher), and *Exploring Our National Historic Parks and Sites,* by Russell D. Butcher. These books feature descriptions and black-and-white photographs of more than 370 National Park System units. Both volumes also contain chapters on possible new parks, threats to the parks, a history of the NPCA, and the national

park standards. To order, contact Roberts Rinehart Publishers, 6309 Monarch Park Place, Niwot, CO 80503; 800-352-1985 or 303-530-4400.

NPCA offers the following brochures at no charge: *The National Parks: How to Have a Quality Experience* and *Visiting Battlefields: The Civil War.* These brochures provide helpful information on how best to enjoy a visit to the national parks. NPCA members can also receive the *Park System Map and Guide, The National Parks Index, The National Parks Camping Guide,* and *Lesser Known Areas* as part of NPCA's PARK-PAK by calling 202-223-6722, ext. 214.

The Story Behind the Scenery® and *The Continuing Story®* series are lavishly illustrated books providing informative text and magnificent photographs of the landscapes, flora, and fauna of our national parklands. More than 100 titles on the national parks, historic events, and Indian cultures, as well as an annual national parks calendar, are available. For information, call toll free 800-626-9673, fax to 702-731-9421, or write to KC Publications, 3245 E. Patrick Lane, Suite A, Las Vegas, NV 89120.

The National Parks: Index and *Lesser Known Areas,* both produced by the National Park Service, can be ordered by contacting the Superintendent of Documents, U.S. Government Printing Office, Washington, DC 20402-9325; 202-512-1800. To receive at no charge the *National Park System Map and Guide,* the *National Trails System Map and Guide;* or an *Official Map and Guide* of specific national parks, contact National Park Service, Office of Information, P.O. Box 37127, Washington, DC 20013-7127; 202-208-4747.

National Parks Visitor Facilities and Services is a directory of vendors authorized to serve park visitors through contracts with the National Park Service. Concessionaires offering lodging, food, beverages, outfitting, tours, trail rides, and other activities and services are listed alphabetically. To order, contact the National Park Hospitality Association, 1331 Pennsylvania Ave., N.W., Suite 724, Washington, DC 20004; 202-662-7097.

Great Walks, Inc., publishes six pocket-sized books of detailed information on specific trails in Yosemite; Sequoia and Kings Canyon in California; Big Bend; Great Smoky Mountains; and Acadia and Mount Desert Island in Maine. For information, send $1 (refundable with your first order) to Great Walks, P.O. Box 410, Goffstown, NH 03045.

The U.S. Bureau of Land Management (BLM) offers free maps that detail recreation areas and scenic and backcountry roads and trails. These are available by contacting the BLM at the Department of the Interior, 1849 C St., N.W., Suite 5600, Washington, DC 20240; 202-452-5125. In addition, *Beyond the National Parks: A Recreational Guide to Public Lands in the West,* published by the Smithsonian Institution Press, is an informative guidebook to many special places administered by the BLM. *America's Secret Recreation Areas,* by Michael Hodgson, is an excellent resource for little-known natural areas in 12 Western states. It details 270 million acres of land administered by BLM, with campgrounds, recreational activities, trails, maps, facilities, and much more. The 1995-96 edition

is published by Foghorn Press and is available for $17.95 by calling 1-800-FOGHORN.

The National Wildlife Refuge Visitors Guide can be ordered free from the U.S. Fish and Wildlife Service's Publications Unit at 4401 North Fairfax Dr., MS 130 Webb, Arlington, VA 22203; 703-358-1711.

The four-volume *Birds of the National Parks,* by Roland H. Wauer, a retired National Park Service (NPS) interpreter and biologist, provides an excellent reference on the parks' birds and their seasons and habitats. This series,

▲ *Prairie at Wind Cave National Park, South Dakota*

written for the average rather than specialist park visitor, is unfortunately out of print.

SAFETY AND REGULATIONS

To protect the national parks' natural and cultural resources and the millions of people who come to enjoy them, the National Park Service asks every visitor to abide by some important regulations. Park staffs do all they can to help you have a safe and pleasant visit, but your cooperation is essential.

Some park hazards—deep lakes, sheer cliffs, extremely hot or cold temperatures—cannot be eliminated. However, accidents and illnesses can be prevented if you use the same common sense you would at home and become familiar with the park. Take some time before your trip or when you first arrive to get to know the park's regulations, warnings, and potential hazards. If you have children, make sure they understand such precautions, and keep a careful watch over them, especially in potentially dangerous situations. If you are injured or become ill, the staff can help by directing you to the nearest medical center and, in some parks, by giving you emergency care.

A few rules and safety tips are common to many parks. At all parks, you must keep your campsite clean and the park free of litter by disposing of refuse in trash receptacles. The National Park Service also asks you to follow federal regulations and refrain from the abuse of alcohol and the use of drugs, which are often contributing factors to injuries and deaths. Other rules and safety tips are outlined in the "Special Advisories and Visitor Ethics" section; more detailed information may be provided in park brochures, on signs, and on bulletin boards at camping areas and other park sites. The National Park Service asks that you report any violation of park regulations to park authorities. If you have any questions, seek the advice of a ranger.

SPECIAL ADVISORIES AND VISITOR ETHICS

Safe Driving

Park roads are designed for sightseeing, not speeding. Because roads are often narrow and winding and sometimes steep, visitors should drive carefully, observe posted speed limits, and be alert for wildlife, pedestrians, bicyclists, other drivers, fallen rocks or trees, slippery roads, and other hazards. Be especially alert

for motorists who might stop unexpectedly for sightseeing or wildlife viewing. Visitors are urged to use roadside pullouts instead of stopping on the roadway.

Campfires

Most parks permit fires, as long as certain rules are followed. To avoid a wildfire that would be dangerous to people, property, and natural resources, parks may allow only certain types of campfires—fires only in grills provided, for example, or in designated fire rings. Firewood gathering may be prohibited or restricted to certain areas, so visitors should plan on bringing their own fuel supply. Fires should be kept under control, should never be left unattended, and should be thoroughly extinguished before departure.

Quiet Hours

Out of respect for other visitors, campers should keep noise to a minimum at all times, especially from 10 p.m. to 6 a.m.

Pets

Pets must always be leashed or otherwise physically restrained for the protection of the animal, other visitors, and wildlife. Pets may be prohibited from certain areas, including public buildings, trails, and the backcountry. A few parks prohibit pets altogether. Dog owners are responsible for keeping their pets quiet in camping areas and elsewhere. Guide dogs are exempted from park restrictions. Some parks provide kennel services; contact the park visitor center for information.

Protection of Valuables

Theft is just as much a problem in the national parks as elsewhere, so when leaving a campsite or heading out on a trail, visitors should take valuables along or hide them out-of-sight in a locked vehicle, preferably in the trunk.

Heat, Cold, and Other Hazards

Visitors should take precautions to deal with the demands and hazards of a park environment. On hot days, pace yourself, schedule strenuous activities for the morning and evening hours, and drink plenty of water and other fluids. On cold days or if you get cold and wet, frostbite and the life-threatening illness called hypothermia can occur, so avoid subjecting yourself to these conditions for long periods. In the thinner air of mountains and high plateaus, even those tasks easy to perform at home can leave one short of breath and dizzy; the best advice is to slow down. If a thunderstorm occurs, avoid exposed areas and open bodies of water, where lightning often strikes, and keep out of low-lying areas and stream beds, where flash floods are most likely to occur.

Wild Plants and Animals

It is the responsibility of every visitor to help preserve the native plants and animals protected in the parks: leave them as you find them, undisturbed and safe. Hunting or carrying a loaded weapon is prohibited in all national parks and national monuments. Hunting during the designated season is allowed in parts of only a few National Park System areas, such as national recreation areas, national preserves, and national seashores and lakeshores. While biting insects or toxic plants, such as poison ivy or poison oak, are the most likely danger you will encounter, visitors should be aware of hazards posed by other wild plants and animals. Rattlesnakes, ticks, and animals carrying rabies or other transmittable diseases, for instance, inhabit some parks. Any wild creature—whether it is as large as a bison or moose or as small as a raccoon or prairie dog—is unpredictable and should be viewed from a distance. Remember that feeding any wild animal is absolutely prohibited.

Campers should especially guard against attracting bears to their campsites as a close encounter with a grizzly, brown, or black bear can result in serious injury or death. Park officials in bear country recommend, and often require, that campers take certain precautions. One is to keep a campsite clean. Bears' sensitive noses can easily detect food left on cans, bottles, and utensils or even personal items with food-like odors (toothpaste, deodorant, etc.). Second, food items should be stored in containers provided by the parks or in your vehicle, preferably out-of-sight in the trunk. Bears, especially those

in Yosemite, are adept at breaking into cars and other motor vehicles containing even small amounts of food and can cause extensive damage to motor vehicles as they attempt to reach what they can smell. Third, in the backcountry, food should be hung from poles or wires that are provided or from a tree; visitors should inquire at the park as to the recommended placement. In treeless surroundings, campers should store food at least 50 yards from any campsite. If bears inhabit a park on your itinerary, ask the National Park Service for a bear brochure with helpful tips on avoiding trouble in bear country and inquire if bears are a problem where you plan to hike or camp.

Backcountry Camping

Camping in the remote backcountry of a park requires much more preparation than other camping. Most parks require that you pick up a backcountry permit before your trip so that rangers will know about your plans. They can also advise you of hazards and regulations and give you up-to-date information on road, trail, river, lake, or sea conditions, weather forecasts, special fire regulations, availability of water, and other matters. Backcountry permits are available at visitor centers, headquarters, and ranger stations.

There are some basic rules to follow whenever you camp in the backcountry: stay on the trails; pack out all trash; obey fire regulations; be prepared for sudden and drastic weather changes; carry a topographic map or nautical chart when necessary; and carry plenty of food and water. In parks where water is either unavailable or scarce, you may need to carry as much as one gallon of water per person per day. In other parks, springs, streams, or lakes may be abundant, but always purify water before drinking it. Untreated water can carry contaminants. One of the most common, especially in Western parks, is *giardia*, an organism that causes an unpleasant intestinal illness. Water may have to be boiled or purified with tablets; check with the park staff for the most effective treatment.

Sanitation

Visitors should bury human waste six to eight inches below ground and a minimum of 100

feet from a watercourse. Waste water should be disposed of at least 100 feet from a watercourse or campsite. Do not wash yourself, your clothing, or your dishes in any watercourse.

CAMPING RESERVATIONS

Most campsites are available on a first-come, first-served basis, but many sites can be reserved through the National Park Reservation Service. For reservations at Acadia, Assateague Island, Cape Hatteras, Channel Islands, Chickasaw, Death Valley, Everglades, Glacier, Grand Canyon, Great Smoky Mountains, Greenbelt, Gulf Islands, Joshua Tree, Katmai, Mount Rainier, Rocky Mountain, Sequoia-Kings Canyon, Sleeping Bear Dunes, Shenandoah, Whiskeytown, and Zion, call 800-365-CAMP. For reservations for Yosemite National Park, call 800-436-PARK. Reservations can also be made at any of these parks in person. Currently, reservations can be made as much as eight weeks in advance or up to the day before the start of a camping stay. Please have credit card and detailed camping information available when you call in order to facilitate the reservation process.

BIOSPHERE RESERVES AND WORLD HERITAGE SITES

A number of the national park units have received international recognition by the United Nations Educational, Scientific and Cultural Organization for their superlative natural and/or cultural values. Biosphere Reserves are representative examples of diverse natural landscapes, with both a fully protected natural core or park unit and surrounding land being managed to meet human needs. World Heritage Sites include natural and cultural sites with "universal" values that illustrate significant geological processes, may be crucial to the survival of threatened plants and animals, or demonstrate outstanding human achievement.

◀ *Eroded formations, Badlands National Park, South Dakota*

CHECKLIST FOR HIKING AND CAMPING

Clothing

Rain gear (jacket and pants)
Windbreaker
Parka
Thermal underwear
T-shirt
Long pants and shorts
Extra wool shirt and/or sweater
Hat with brim
Hiking boots
Camp shoes/sneakers
Wool mittens
Lightweight shoes

Equipment

First-aid kit
Pocket knife
Sunglasses
Sunscreen
Topographic map
Compass
Flashlight, fresh batteries, spare bulb
Extra food and water (even for short hikes)
Waterproof matches

Fire starter
Candles
Toilet paper
Digging tool for toilet needs
Day backpack
Sleeping bag
Sleeping pad or air mattress
Tarp/ground sheet
Sturdy tent, preferably free-standing
Insect repellent
Lip balm
Pump-type water filter/water purification tablets
Water containers
Plastic trash bags
Biodegradable soap
Small towel
Toothbrush
Lightweight backpack stove/extra fuel
Cooking pot(s)
Eating utensils
Can opener
Electrolyte replacement for plain water (e.g., Gatorade)
Camera, film, lenses, filters
Binoculars
Sewing kit
Lantern
Nylon cord (50 feet)
Whistle
Signal mirror

A Brief History

▲ *Cannonball concretions, Theodore Roosevelt National Park, North Dakota*

A Brief History of the National Parks and Conservation Association

In 1916, when Congress established the National Park Service to administer the then nearly 40 national parks and monuments, the agency's first director, Stephen Tyng Mather, quickly saw the need for a private organization, independent of the federal government, to be the citizens' advocate for the parks.

Consequently, on May 19, 1919, the National Parks Association—later renamed the National Parks and Conservation Association (NPCA)—was founded in Washington, D.C. The National Park Service's former public relations director, Robert Sterling Yard, was named to lead the new organization—a position he held for a quarter century.

The association's chief objectives were then and continue to be the following: to vigorously oppose threats to the integrity of the parks; to advocate worthy and consistent standards of *national* significance for the addition of new units to the National Park System; and, through a variety of educational means, to promote the public understanding and appreciation of the parks. From the beginning, threats to the parks have been a major focus of the organization. One of the biggest conservation battles of NPCA's earliest years erupted in 1920, when Montana irrigation interests advocated building a dam and raising the level of Yellowstone Lake in Yellowstone National Park. Fortunately, this threat to the world's first national park was ultimately defeated—the first landmark victory of the fledgling citizens' advocacy group on behalf of the national parks.

At about the same time, a controversy developed over the authority given to the Water Power Commission (later renamed the Federal Power Commission) to authorize the construction of hydropower projects in national parks. The commission had already approved the flooding of Hetch Hetchy Valley in Yosemite National Park. In the ensuing political struggle, NPCA pushed for an amendment to the water power law that would prohibit such projects in

all national parks. A compromise produced only a partial victory: the ban applied to the parks then in existence, but not to parks yet to be established. As a result, each new park's enabling legislation would have to expressly stipulate that the park was exempt from the commission's authority to develop hydropower projects. Yet this success, even if partial, was significant.

Also in the 1920s, NPCA successfully urged establishment of new national parks: Shenandoah, Great Smoky Mountains, Carlsbad Caverns, Bryce Canyon, and a park that later became Kings Canyon, as well as an expanded Sequoia. The association also pushed to expand Yellowstone, Grand Canyon, and Rocky Mountain national parks, pointing out that "the boundaries of the older parks were often established arbitrarily, following ruler lines drawn in far-away offices." The association continues to advocate such topographically and ecologically oriented boundary improvements for many parks.

In 1930, the establishment of Colonial National Historical Park and the George Washington Birthplace National Monument signaled a broadening of the National Park System to places of primarily historical rather than environmental importance. A number of other historical areas, such as Civil War battlefields, were soon transferred from U.S. military jurisdiction to the National Park Service, and NPCA accurately predicted that this new category of parks "will rapidly surpass, in the number of units, its world-celebrated scenic" parks. Today, there are roughly 200 historical parks out of the total of 378 units. NPCA also pushed to add other units, including Everglades National Park, which was finally established in 1947.

A new category of National Park System units was initiated with the establishment of Cape Hatteras National Seashore in North Carolina. However, in spite of NPCA opposition, Congress permitted public hunting in the seashore—a precedent that subsequently opened the way to allow this consumptive resource use in other national seashores, national lakeshores, national rivers, and national preserves. With the exception of traditional, subsistence hunting in Alaska national preserves, NPCA continues to oppose hunting in all national parks and monuments.

In contrast to its loss at Cape Hatteras, NPCA achieved a victory regarding Kings Canyon National Park as a result of patience and tenacity. When the park was established in 1940, two valleys—Tehipite and Cedar Grove—were left out of the park as a concession to hydroelectric power and irrigation interests. A few years later, however, as the result of concerted efforts by the association and other environmental groups, these magnificently scenic valleys were added to the park.

In 1942, the association took a major step in its public education mission when it began publishing *National Parks*. This award-winning, full-color magazine contains news, editorials, and feature articles that help to inform members about the parks, threats facing them, and opportunities for worthy new parks and offers readers a chance to participate in the protection and enhancement of the National Park System.

In one of the most heavily publicized park-protection battles of the 1950s, NPCA and other groups succeeded in blocking construction of two hydroelectric power dams that would have inundated the spectacularly scenic river canyons in Dinosaur National Monument. In the 1960s, an even bigger battle erupted over U.S. Bureau of Reclamation plans to build two dams in the Grand Canyon. But with the cooperative efforts of a number of leading environmental organizations and tremendous help from the news media, these schemes were defeated, and Grand Canyon National Park was expanded.

In 1980, the National Park System nearly tripled in size with the passage of the Alaska National Interest Lands Conservation Act (ANILCA). One of the great milestones in the history of American land conservation, ANILCA established ten new, and expanded three existing, national park units in Alaska. This carefully crafted compromise also recognized the special circumstances of Alaska and authorized subsistence hunting, fishing, and gathering by rural residents as well as special access provisions on most units. The challenge of ANILCA is to achieve a balance of interests that are often in conflict. Currently, NPCA is working to protect sensitive park areas and wildlife from inappropriate development of roads and unregulated motorized use, and to ensure that our magnificent national parks in Alaska

always offer the sense of wildness, discovery, and adventure that Congress intended.

In 1981, the association sponsored a conference to address serious issues affecting the welfare of the National Park System. The following year, NPCA published a book on this theme called *National Parks in Crisis*. In the 1980s and 1990s, as well, the association sponsored its nationwide "March for Parks" program in conjunction with Earth Day in April. Money raised from the hundreds of marches funds local park projects, including improvement and protection priorities and educational projects in national, state, and local parks.

NPCA's landmark nine-volume document, *National Park System Plan*, was issued in 1988. It contained proposals for new parks and park expansions, assessments of threats to park resources and of research needs, explorations of the importance of interpretation to the visitor's quality of experience, and issues relating to the internal organization of the National Park Service. Two years later, the two-volume *Visitor Impact Management* was released. This document found favor within the National Park Service because of its pragmatic discussions of "carrying capacity" and visitor-impact management methodology and its case studies. In 1993, *Park Waters in Peril* was released, focusing on threats seriously jeopardizing water resources and presenting a dozen case studies.

The association has become increasingly concerned about the effect of noise on the natural quiet in the parks. NPCA has helped formulate restrictions on flightseeing tours over key parts of the Grand Canyon; urged special restrictions on tour flights over Alaska's national parks; supported a ban on tour flights over other national parks such as Yosemite; expressed opposition to plans for construction of major new commercial airports close to Mojave National Preserve and Petroglyph National Monument; opposed the recreational use of snowmobiles in some parks and advocated restrictions on their use in others; and supported regulations prohibiting the use of personal watercraft on lakes in national parks.

Other association activities of the late 20th century have included helping to block development of a major gold mining operation that could have seriously impaired Yellowstone National Park; opposing a coal mine near

Zion National Park that would have polluted Zion Canyon's North Fork of the Virgin River; objecting to proposed lead mining that could pollute the Ozark National Scenic Riverways; opposing a major waste dump adjacent to Joshua Tree National Park; and helping to defeat a proposed U.S. Department of Energy nuclear waste dump adjacent to Canyonlands National Park and on lands worthy of addition to the park. NPCA is currently proposing the completion of this national park with the addition of 500,000 acres. This proposal to double the size of the park would extend protection across the entire Canyonlands Basin. NPCA has also continued to work with the Everglades Coalition and others to help formulate meaningful ways of restoring the seriously impaired Everglades ecosystem; is urging protection of New Mexico's geologically and scenically outstanding Valles Caldera, adjacent to Bandelier National Monument; and is pushing for the installation of scrubbers on air-polluting coal-fired power plants in the Midwest and upwind from the Grand Canyon.

The association, in addition, is continuing to seek meaningful solutions to traffic congestion and urbanization on the South Rim of the Grand Canyon and in Yosemite Valley; is opposing construction of a six-lane highway through Petroglyph National Monument that would destroy sacred Native American cultural assets; and is fighting a plan to build a new road through Denali National Park. NPCA has supported re-establishment of such native wildlife as the gray wolf at Yellowstone and desert bighorn sheep at Capitol Reef and other desert parks, as well as urging increased scientific research that will enable the National Park Service to more effectively protect natural ecological processes in the future. The association is also continuing to explore a proposal to combine Organ Pipe Cactus National Monument and Cabreza Prieta National Wildlife Refuge into a Sonoran Desert National Park, possibly in conjunction with Mexico's Pinacate Biosphere Reserve.

In 1994, on the occasion of NPCA's 75th anniversary, the association sponsored a major conference on the theme "Citizens Protecting America's Parks: Joining Forces for the Future." As a result, NPCA became more active in recruiting a more racially and socially diverse group of park protectors. Rallying new constituencies for the parks helped NPCA in 1995 to defeat a bill that would have called for Congress to review national parks for possible closure. NPCA was also instrumental in the passage of legislation to establish the National Underground Railroad Network to Freedom.

In January 1999, NPCA hosted another major conference, this time focusing on the need for the park system, and the Park Service itself, to be relevant, accessible, and open to all Americans. The conference led to the creation of a number of partnership teams between national parks and minority communities. In conjunction with all this program activity, the association experienced its greatest growth in membership, jumping from about 24,000 in 1980 to nearly 400,000 in the late 1990s.

As NPCA and its committed Board of Trustees, staff, and volunteers face the challenges of park protection in the 21st century, the words of the association's past president, Wallace W. Atwood, in 1929 are as timely now as then:

> All who join our association have the satisfaction that comes only from unselfish acts; they will help carry forward a consistent and progressive program . . . for the preservation and most appropriate utilization of the unique wonderlands of our country. Join and make this work more effective.

Each of us can help nurture one of the noblest endeavors in the entire history of mankind—the national parks idea that began so many years ago at Yellowstone and has spread and blossomed around the world. Everyone can help make a difference in determining just how well we succeed in protecting the priceless and irreplaceable natural and cultural heritage of the National Park System and passing it along unimpaired for the generations to come.

Apostle Islands National Lakeshore

▲ *Caves at Squaw Bay*

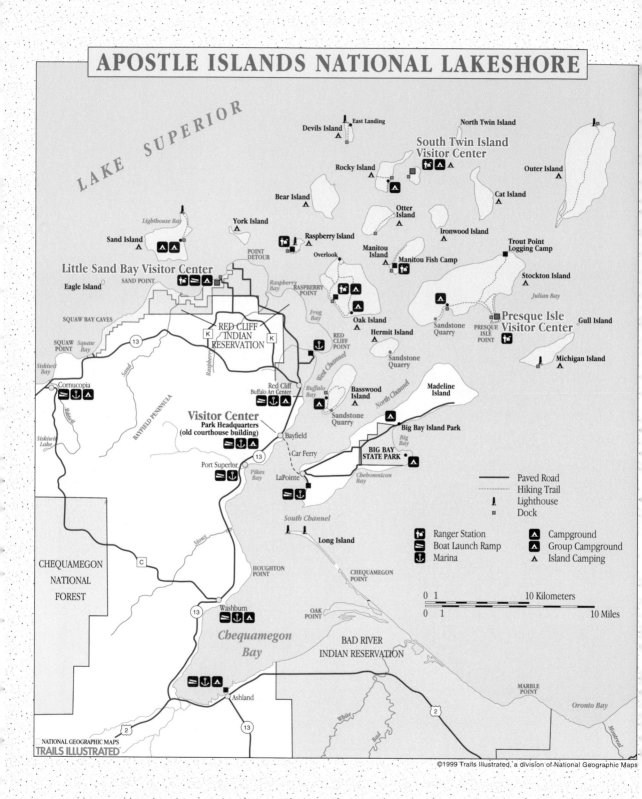

APOSTLE ISLANDS NATIONAL LAKESHORE

LAKE SUPERIOR

Devils Island
East Landing

North Twin Island

South Twin Island
Visitor Center

Rocky Island

Outer Island

Bear Island

Cat Island

Otter Island

Lighthouse Bay

York Island

Raspberry Island

Ironwood Island

Sand Island

Overlook

Manitou Island

Manitou Fish Camp

Trout Point
Logging Camp

POINT DETOUR

Little Sand Bay Visitor Center

SAND POINT

Raspberry Bay

RASPBERRY POINT

Stockton Island

Julian Bay

Eagle Island

Frog Bay

Oak Island

Hermit Island

Sandstone Quarry

Presque Isle
Visitor Center

Gull Island

SQUAW BAY CAVES

RED CLIFF
INDIAN
RESERVATION

K   K

RED CLIFF POINT

PRESQUE ISLE POINT

SQUAW POINT

Squaw Bay

Sand

Sandstone Quarry

Michigan Island

Siskiwit Bay

Cornucopia

Red Cliff
Buffalo Art Center

Buffalo Bay

Basswood Island

West Channel

Madeline Island

BAYFIELD PENINSULA

Siskiwit Lake

Visitor Center
Park Headquarters
(old courthouse building)

Bayfield

Sandstone Quarry

North Channel

Big Bay Island Park

Big Bay

BIG BAY
STATE PARK

Port Superior

Pikes Bay

Car Ferry

LaPointe

Chebomnicon Bay

Paved Road
Hiking Trail

Sioux

South Channel

Long Island

Lighthouse
Dock

Ranger Station
Boat Launch Ramp
Marina

Campground
Group Campground
Island Camping

CHEQUAMEGON
NATIONAL
FOREST

C

HOUGHTON POINT

CHEQUAMEGON POINT

0   1   10 Kilometers
0   1   10 Miles

Washburn

OAK POINT

Chequamegon Bay

BAD RIVER
INDIAN RESERVATION

MARBLE POINT

Ashland

White

Bad

Oronto Bay

Montreal

NATIONAL GEOGRAPHIC MAPS
TRAILS ILLUSTRATED

©1999 Trails Illustrated, a division of National Geographic Maps

Apostle Islands National Lakeshore

Route 1, Box 4
Bayfield, WI 54814-9599
715-779-3397

Established in 1970, this 69,371-acre national lakeshore protects 21 richly forested islands in Lake Superior and more than ten miles of scenic sandstone cliffs, "sea" caves, bluffs, and beaches along the northern shore of Bayfield Peninsula in northwest Wisconsin. The island, mainland, wetlands, and lake habitats support a great variety of flora and fauna and provide a wide variety of recreational opportunities.

OUTSTANDING FEATURES

Among the many outstanding features of the park are the following: **Stockton Island**, the national lakeshore's largest island, providing two docks, a visitor center, hiking trails, and picnicking and camping facilities; **Raspberry Island Lighthouse**, one of the lakeshore's six 19th-century light stations that remain in operation (guided tours are given in the summer); **Manitou Island Fish Camp**, the restored site of a historic, commercial fish camp (open in summer); and **Hokenson Brothers Fishery**, a group of historic buildings that comprised a family fishing business from the late 1920s to the early 1960s on the mainland near the Little Sand Bay Visitor Center; the fishery includes a twine shed, in which fishing artifacts are exhibited, and offers interpreted self-guided and guided tours in the summer.

PRACTICAL INFORMATION

When to Go

The national lakeshore is open year-round although summer and autumn are the most popular seasons to visit. Summer temperatures average 75-80 degrees in the day and 55 degrees at night. Beautiful autumn foliage peaks from mid-September through early October. Spring is often damp and cold, with sudden changes in the weather. Winter activities are becoming increasingly popular, although far-below-zero bitter cold and strong winds are common, with as much as 100 inches of annual snowfall.

How to Get There

By Car: From U.S. Route 2 at Ashland, drive west three miles on U.S. Route 2 and north 20 miles on State Route 13 to Bayfield, where the national lakeshore's main visitor center is located in the Old Bayfield County Courthouse building on Washington Avenue between 4th and 5th streets.

By Air: Duluth International Airport (218-727-2968) is served by Northwest Airlines and United Express.

By Train: Amtrak (800-872-7245) has stops in Milwaukee and Winona, Wisconsin, and Red Wing, Minnesota.

By Bus: Greyhound Lines (800-231-2222) has stops in Ashland, Wisconsin.

By Boat: Apostle Islands Cruise Service (715-779-3925 or 800-323-7619) offers daily sightseeing tours of the islands during summer months. Apostle Islands Water Taxi (715-779-5153 or 800-323-7619) provides service from Bayfield to island points for up to six passengers. Charter boats and boat rentals are also available.

Fees and Permits

No entrance fee is charged. Free permits, available at visitor centers, are required for camping and scuba diving; both types are available at the visitor center. A Wisconsin fishing license with a Great Lakes trout and salmon stamp is required for fishing.

Visitor Centers and Museum

Bayfield Visitor Center: open daily from May through mid-October, and weekdays from mid-October through April; closed Thanksgiving, Christmas, and New Year's Day. Interpretive exhibits, orientation film, publications, maps, and permits.

Little Sand Bay Visitor Center: open daily from early June to early September, and Fridays through Sundays from early through late September. Interpretive exhibits, audiovisual program, publications, and permits.

Presque Isle Visitor Center, on Stockton Island: open in summer only, staffed intermittently. Self-guided interpretive information.

South Twin Island Visitor Center: open in summer only.

Facilities

Available are docks, marinas, and boat-launching ramps, along with trails, picnic areas, and designated campsites.

Handicapped Accessibility

Bayfield Visitor Center, Apostle Islands Cruise Service excursion boat, Stockton Island Visitor Center, and the Manitou Fish Camp are wheelchair-accessible.

Medical Services

First aid is available at ranger stations. The closest hospital is in Ashland, about 25 miles from Bayfield.

Pets

Pets must be leashed and under control at all times. Leashes may not exceed six feet. Pets are not permitted on excursion boats.

Safety and Regulations

For your safety and enjoyment and for the protection of the park, please follow these regulations and suggestions:

- Lake Superior waters are dangerously cold, and sudden storms are common, so the National Park Service advises that visitors understand what hypothermia is and how to avoid and treat it. It is important for those on the water to obtain current weather information from the National Park Service or U.S. Coast Guard before setting out on Lake Superior.

- Divers must display a dive flag.

- Refuge areas are closed to fishing.

- Filter, boil, or treat all water before drinking.

- Caution is urged near the brink of cliffs, as rocks may be loose and slippery.

- It is always wise to inform a park ranger of your backcountry plans.

- In winter, over-ice travel is permitted, but extreme caution is recommended because of unpredictable and hazardous conditions.

- Swim at your own risk; no lifeguards are on duty within the national lakeshore.

- All natural, historic, and cultural features are protected and are to be left undisturbed.

- Please respect and do not trespass on private properties that are scattered within the national lakeshore.

The National Park Service asks that visitors not litter the park. Remember the excellent slogan to "leave only footprints" as a guide to help protect this national park.

ACTIVITIES

Options include interpretive tours, boat cruises, boating, kayaking, sailing, hiking, birdwatching, picnicking, camping, bog and beach walks, campfire programs, guest lectures, scuba diving, fishing, cross-country skiing, snow-shoeing, ice fishing, and public hunting in part of the lakeshore during the designated season. Also located within the national lakeshore is the Indiana Dunes Environmental Learning Center. This is a year-round residential complex focusing on environmental education for students. The Learning Center is operated in partnership with a private not-for-profit organization, the Indiana Dunes Environmental Learning Center, Inc. For more information about the center call 219-395-9555. Additional details about other activities are provided in the lakeshore's newspaper, *Around the Archipelago*.

Hiking Trails

Among the many trails available are the following:

On the mainland: **Lakeshore Trail**, a fairly easy, two-mile route beginning at the Meyers Road picnic area near the west end of the lakeshore's mainland unit, and providing spectacular views of Squaw Bay "sea" caves from the top of Lake Superior cliffs; in 1999, the six-mile stretch of the trail from there to the tip of Sand Point is not yet complete.

On the islands: **South Twin Island Trail**, an easy quarter-mile route, beginning at the visitor center; and **Stockton Island Trail**, fairly easy routes totaling 14 miles beginning at the visitor center, encircling Presque Isle Point, and branching off to Trout Point Logging Camp and to a historic sandstone quarry.

Other hiking trails are located on Basswood, Oak, Manitou, Raspberry, Sand, Otter, Rocky, Devils, and Outer islands.

OVERNIGHT STAYS

Lodging and Dining

The national lakeshore has no overnight or dining facilities. Nearby communities, such as Bayfield, La Pointe, Washburn, and Ashland, offer lodgings, restaurants, service stations, and stores.

Camping

Camping is permitted on 18 of the 21 islands at designated campsites and in the backcountry. Campsite reservations can be made by calling 715-779-3397. Free permits, available at visitor centers, are required. Campers in need of transportation can reach five of the islands on regularly scheduled cruises from late June to Labor Day. A water taxi is available to carry campers to the less-visited islands. Visitors are urged to practice minimum-impact and bear-country camping techniques. Tent sites are available on the following islands with a 14-day limit: Basswood, Devils, Manitou, Oak, Rocky, Sand, South Twin, and Stockton

islands. Drinking water is available from mid-May through September on Basswood, Oak, Rocky, Sand, South Twin, and Stockton islands. Most sites are for parties of fewer than seven persons; larger group sites (reservations required) are available at Basswood, Oak, Sand, and Stockton islands. Camping outside of designated areas is possible on most islands.

FLORA AND FAUNA (Partial Listings)

Mammals: moose, whitetail deer, bobcat, coyote, red fox, mink, river otter, longtail weasel, beaver, muskrat, woodchuck, porcupine, raccoon, striped skunk, eastern cottontail, red squirrel, and eastern and least chipmunks.

Birds: common loon, double-crested cormorant, great blue heron, Canada goose, mallard, black duck, lesser scaup, common goldeneye, red-breasted and common mergansers, goshawk, hawks (sharp-shinned, red-tailed, and broad-winged), bald eagle, osprey, ruffed grouse, spotted sandpiper, herring and ring-billed gulls, mourning dove, great horned and barred owls, chimney swift, belted kingfisher, flicker, woodpeckers (pileated, hairy, and downy), yellow-bellied sapsucker, eastern kingbird, least flycatcher, swallows (tree, barn, and cliff), blue jay, raven, crow, black-capped chickadee, white-breasted and red-breasted nuthatches, winter wren, robin, thrushes (wood, hermit, and Swainson's), veery, ruby-crowned and golden-crowned kinglets, cedar waxwing, red-eyed vireo, warblers (black-and-white, Nashville, parula, yellow, magnolia, Cape May, black-throated blue, yellow-rumped, black-throated green, blackburnian, chestnut-sided, pine, palm, and Canada), ovenbird, common yellowthroat, American redstart, red-winged blackbird, Baltimore oriole, scarlet tanager, rose-breasted and evening grosbeaks, common redpoll, pine siskin, American goldfinch, red and white-winged crossbills, dark-eyed junco, and tree, chipping, song, and white-throated sparrows.

Trees, Shrubs, and Flowers: pines (white, red, and jack), tamarack, white and black spruces, eastern hemlock, balsam fir, eastern white cedar, northern red oak, yellow and paper birches, speckled alder, American basswood, balsam poplar, quaking and bigtooth aspens, willows, common chokecherry, Canada plum, pin cherry, mountain ash, maples (mountain, red, and sugar), green and black ashes, American yew, common ground juniper, beaked hazelnut, sweetgale, meadowsweet, juneberries, thimbleberry, blackberry, raspberry, currants, wild and swamp roses, beach heath, red-osier dogwood, labrador tea, swamp laurel, bog rosemary, leatherleaf, creeping snowberry, bearberry, cranberries (highbush, large, and small), huckleberry, blueberries, trailing arbutus, pipsissewa, wintergreen, partridgeberry, elderberries, staghorn sumac, bloodroot, bunchberry, Canada mayflower, clintonia, goldthread, orange and Canada hawkweeds, jack-in-the-pulpit, marsh marigold, pink ladies'-slipper, skunk cabbage, false Solomon's seal, starflower, wood anemone, beach pea, black-eyed Susan, iris, evening primrose, fire-weed, goldenrods, pitcher plant, sundews, shinleaf, Joe-pye-weed, common St. Johnswort, swamp candle, and asters.

NEARBY POINTS OF INTEREST

The area surrounding this lakeshore offers other fascinating attractions that can be enjoyed as day trips or overnight excursions. Big Bay State Park is located on Madeline Island, the largest of the Apostle Islands, but not part of the national lakeshore. Isle Royale National Park is to the northeast in Lake Superior; Keweenaw National Historical Park, Porcupine Mountains State Park, and Pictured Rocks National Lakeshore are to the east in Michigan's Upper Peninsula; Chequamegon National Forest is to the south in Wisconsin; and Grand Portage National Monument and Voyageurs National Park are to the northwest in Minnesota.

By Bus: ALSI Airport Shuttle (605-343-5358) offers four-hour, round-trip tours from Rapid City through Badlands National Park.

Fees and Permits

Entrance fees, valid for seven consecutive days, are $10 per vehicle or $5 per person on foot or bicycle. Commercial vehicles pay acording to passenger size of the vehicle. Permits are not required for backcountry excursions, but registration is advisable for safety reasons.

Visitor Centers

Ben Reifel Visitor Center: open daily. Call 605-433-5361 for hours of operation. Interpretive exhibits, programs, publications, maps, and schedules.

White River Visitor Center, on the Pine Ridge Reservation: open daily, June through late August. Call 605-433-5361 for hours of operation. Interpretive exhibits, audiovisual program, and publications.

Handicapped Accessibility

Visitor centers, amphitheater, some sites in Cedar Pass Campground, Fossil Exhibit Trail, Bigfoot Picnic Area, Window Trail, most overlooks, the Cedar Pass Lodge gift shop and dining room, and a cabin at Cedar Pass Lodge are wheelchair-accessible. Ben Reifel Visitor Center has an open-captioned orientation film and a "touch room" where exhibits can be handled.

Medical Services

First aid is available at ranger stations. The closest hospital is in Philip, 35 miles away. Medical facilities are available in Wall, Kadoka, and Rapid City.

Pets

Pets must be leashed or otherwise physically restrained at all times, and leashes may not exceed six feet. Pets are not permitted in the Sage Creek Wilderness.

Climate

The Badlands climate is characterized by unpredictability. Heavy rain, hail, and strong winds are possible. Lightning strikes are common, and visitors are strongly advised to stay away from ridges, exposed places, or isolated trees during thunderstorms. Average daily temperature range in Fahrenheit and average daily precipitation are as follows:

	AVERAGE DAILY	
Month	**Temperature F**	**Precipitation**
January	11-34°	0.3 inches
February	16-40°	0.5 inches
March	24-48°	0.9 inches
April	36-62°	1.8 inches
May	46-72°	2.8 inches
June	56-83°	3.1 inches
July	62-92°	1.9 inches
August	61-91°	1.5 inches
September	51-81°	1.2 inches
October	39-68°	0.9 inches
November	26-48°	0.4 inches
December	17-39°	0.3 inches

Safety and Regulations

For your safety and enjoyment and for the protection of the park, please follow these regulations and suggestions:

- Visitors are urged to be alert for prairie rattlesnakes and to keep a safe distance from bison (at least 100 yards) as their behavior is unpredictable and they can run up to 30 mph.

- Hikers are advised to stay a safe distance back from sheer drop-offs and avoid steep slopes, which are unstable and can easily give way under foot.

- Campers are not permitted to build campfires in the park; camp stoves may be used.

- Lightning, hail, strong winds, and intensely hot sun require caution in summer.

▲ *Badlands landscape at moonrise, Badlands National Park, South Dakota*

- Park waters are not potable; even boiling, filtering, or treating it does not make it fit for human consumption.

- Especially in the summer, hikers are advised to carry at least one gallon of water per day per person.

- Remember that feeding, disturbing, capturing, and hunting wildlife, as well as disturbing or removing fossils and damaging vegetation, are all illegal.

The National Park Service asks that visitors not litter the park. Remember the excellent slogan to "leave only footprints" as a guide to help protect this national park.

ACTIVITIES

Options include hiking, scenic drives, bird-watching, ranger-led interpretive talks and walks, evening campfire programs, night walks, interpretive presentations on fossils, picnicking, camping, and bicycling. Further information is provided in the park's newspaper, *The Prairie Preamble.*

Hiking Trails

Along State Route 240, known as the Badlands Loop Road, which winds for 30 miles along the Badlands Wall in the park's North Unit, many pullouts and overlooks offer spectacular views of the Badlands. The trails described below begin at this route. Note that the Badlands (Sage Creek) Wilderness has no established trails.

Trails starting at Route 240 include the following: **Fossil Exhibit Trail**, an easy and very popular, quarter-mile, self-guided interpretive, wheelchair-accessible loop beginning and ending at the top of Norbeck Pass on the Badlands Loop Drive and leading through fossil exhibits; **Cliff Shelf Nature Trail**, a fairly easy, half-mile loop beginning and ending a half-mile northeast of Ben Reifel Visitor Center and leading through an ecologically interesting area of juniper trees, badlands, prairie grasslands, and cattail-bordered sinkholes; **Window Trail**, an easy eighth-of-a-mile, wheelchair-accessible route beginning at the middle of the Doors and Windows parking area and leading to a view of a natural eroded "window" in the Badlands Wall and a canyon; **Door Trail**, an easy .3-mile, self-guided interpretive route beginning at the north end of the large Doors and Windows parking area, passing through a "doorway" (an eroded notch) in the Badlands Wall, and providing excellent views of rugged badlands formations; **Notch Trail**, a moderately to fairly strenuous, .75-mile route (wearing hiking boots and carrying water are advised), beginning at the south end of the Doors and Windows parking area, leading along a stretch of ledge, and providing a grand panorama of the White River Valley— a trail not recommended for hikers fearful of heights; **Saddle Pass Trail**, a strenuous, .75-mile route beginning from a parking area two miles northwest of Ben Reifel Visitor Center on the Badlands Loop Drive, then climbing (steeply in places) through the banded sedimentary formations of the Badlands Wall and linking up with the Castle and Medicine Root trails; and **Castle Trail**, a fairly easy, mostly level, 5.25-mile route (carrying water is advised), between the Doors and Windows parking area and the Fossil Exhibit parking area, paralleling the rim of the Badlands Wall, and leading through a mixed-grass prairie. The Medicine Root Trail enables hikers to make a loop with the Castle Trail.

The National Park Service advises that visitors planning excursions into the wilderness should use a topographic map and discuss routes with a ranger.

OVERNIGHT STAYS

Lodging and Dining

Cedar Pass Lodge, near the Ben Reifel Visitor Center and park headquarters, is open from mid-April to late October. Cabins dating from the 1930s and remodeled in the late 1980s, a restaurant (open from mid-March to late October), and gift shop. For reservations, contact the lodge at Box 5, Interior, SD 57750; 605-433-5460.

Lodging Outside the Park

Interior, Wall, and Rapid City are among nearby communities providing accommodations, restaurants, service stations, and other facilities.

▲ *Buffalo skull and eroded formations, Badlands National Park, South Dakota*

Campgrounds

Campgrounds are open year-round on a first-come, first-served basis. Visitors are advised to check weather conditions and possible closings prior to arrival. Cedar Pass has water and flush toilets in the summer. During the rest of the year, water is not available, but vault toilets are provided. Group camping is permitted year-round. Reservations are required for group camping between Memorial Day and Labor Day (and are accepted the rest of the year). To make reservations, contact park headquarters.

Backcountry Camping

Camping in the backcountry is allowed year-round throughout much of the park on a first-come, first-served basis. Permits are not required, and campers may camp anywhere as long as they are out of view of roads and trails. No water is potable in the backcountry, so all water must be carried from outside sources. One gallon per person per day is the suggested minimum. All cooking must be done with camp stoves since open flames are prohibited because of the risk of fire.

FLORA AND FAUNA (Partial Listings)

Mammals: bison (buffalo), mule and whitetail deer, bighorn sheep, pronghorn, mountain lion, bobcat, coyote, red and swift foxes, badger, porcupine, raccoon, striped skunk, black-footed ferret, longtail weasel, whitetail jackrabbit, blacktail prairie dog, desert cottontail, thirteen-lined ground squirrel, and badlands chipmunk.

Birds: pied-billed grebe, Canada goose, mallard, green-winged teal, northern harrier, red-tailed and Swainson's hawks, golden eagle, kestrel, prairie falcon, turkey vulture, sharp-tailed grouse, killdeer, upland sandpiper, mourning dove, burrowing and long-eared owls, white-throated swift, flicker, Says' phoebe, eastern and western kingbirds, horned lark, swallows (northern rough-winged, cliff, and barn), black-billed magpie, crow, blue jay, black-capped chickadee, rock wren, mountain bluebird, Townsend's solitaire, robin, brown thrasher, loggerhead shrike, warblers (yellow-rumped, orange-crowned, yellow, and yellowthroat), American redstart, yellow-breasted chat, spotted towhee, sparrows (chipping, grasshopper, and lark), lark bunting, chestnut-collared longspur, red-winged blackbird, western meadowlark, Bullock's and orchard orioles, gray-crowned rosy finch, and redpoll.

Amphibians and Reptiles: northern leopard and western chorus frogs, Woodhouse's and great plains toads, bullsnake, yellow-bellied racer, and prairie rattlesnake.

Trees, Shrubs, Flowers, and Grasses: ponderosa pine (very few), Rocky Mountain juniper, American and slippery elms, plains cottonwood, willows, common chokecherry, boxelder, green ash, rabbitbrush, four-winged saltbush, greasewood, buffaloberry, skunkbush sumac, currants, coralberries, sagebrushes, Rocky Mountain sage (salvia), snow-on-the-mountain, poison ivy, wild rose, cattail, shrubby cinquefoil, blazingstar, milk-vetches, locoweeds, iris, blue-eyed grass, Hood and plains phlox, kinnikinnick, pasqueflower, prickly poppy, prairie golden-pea, milkweeds, prairie turnip, scarlet globemallow, sego and mariposa lilies, bluebell, Indian paintbrush, penstemons, Easter daisy, evening primrose, spiderwort, dotted gayfeather, sunflowers, upright prairie and short-ray coneflowers, goldenrods, prairie asters, western wallflower, bladderpods, soapweed yucca, and prickly pear, hedgehog, and pincushion cacti. Of the tall grasses, there are big bluestem, prairie cordgrass, and switchgrass; of the medium grasses, there are Indian ricegrass, needle-and-thread, western and crested wheatgrasses, little bluestem, and side-oats grama; and of the short grasses, there are blue and hairy gramas, red threeawn, and buffalograss.

NEARBY POINTS OF INTEREST

The area surrounding Badlands National Park offers a number of additional natural and historic attractions that can be enjoyed as day trips or overnight excursions. Adjacent to the park are Buffalo Gap National Grassland and the Pine Ridge Reservation, the site of the Wounded Knee Massacre Monument. To the west in the Black Hills are Wind Cave National Park, Mount Rushmore National Memorial, Jewel Cave National Monument, and Custer State Park. Agate Fossil Beds National Monument is to the southwest in Nebraska.

Indiana Dunes National Lakeshore

▲ Mount Baldy

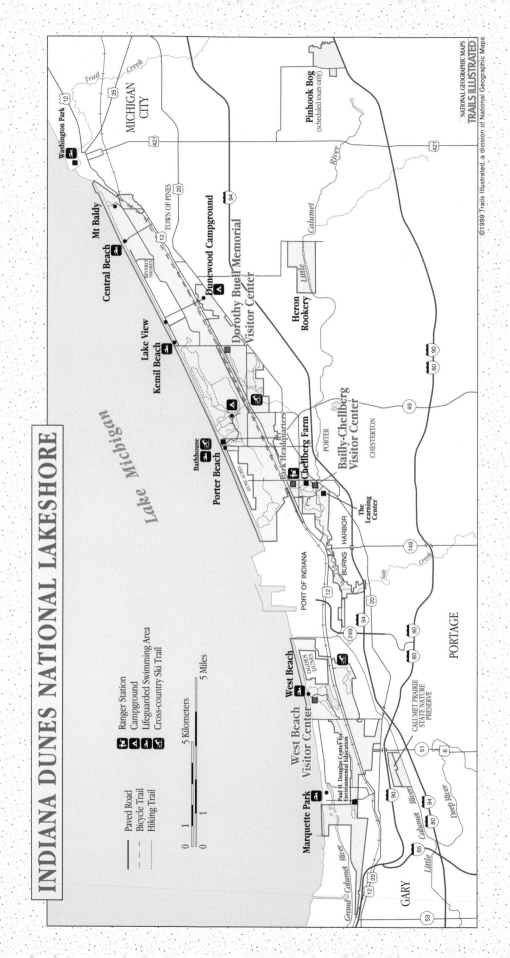

INDIANA DUNES NATIONAL LAKESHORE

Lake Michigan

Legend

—— Paved Road
– – – Bicycle Trail
········· Hiking Trail

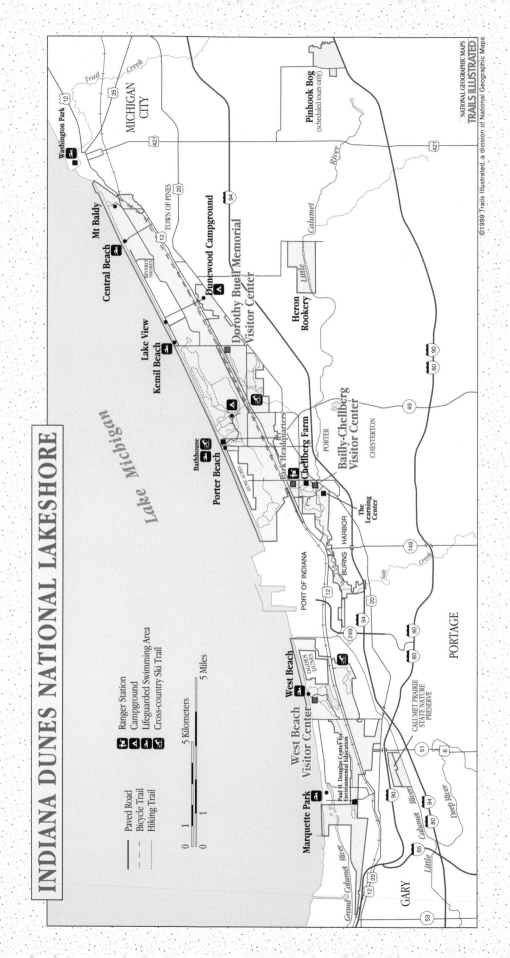 Ranger Station
 Campground
 Lifeguarded Swimming Area
 Cross-country Ski Trail

0 1 5 Kilometers
0 1 5 Miles

Washington Park

MICHIGAN CITY

Mt Baldy

Central Beach

Lake View

Kemil Beach

BEVERLY SHORES

TOWN OF PINES

Dunewood Campground

Dorothy Buell Memorial Visitor Center

Heron Rookery

Little Calumet River

Pinhook Bog
(scheduled tours only)

Bathhouse

Porter Beach

DUNE ACRES

Park Headquarters

Chellberg Farm

Bailly-Chellberg Visitor Center

PORTER

CHESTERTON

The Learning Center

HARBOR

BURNS

PORT OF INDIANA

Salt Creek

West Beach

OGDEN DUNES

West Beach Visitor Center

Marquette Park

Paul H. Douglas Center for Environmental Education

CALUMET PRAIRIE STATE NATURE PRESERVE

PORTAGE

Grand Calumet River

Little Calumet River

Deep River

GARY

NATIONAL GEOGRAPHIC MAPS
TRAILS ILLUSTRATED

©1999 Trails Illustrated, a division of National Geographic Maps

Indiana Dunes National Lakeshore

**1100 North Mineral Springs Road
Porter, IN 46304-1299
219-926-7561**

This 15,139-acre national lakeshore at the southern end of Lake Michigan between Gary and Michigan City, Indiana, protects several sections of an ecologically rich area of scenic sand dunes, stretches of sandy beaches, inter-dunal ponds, marshes, bogs, swamps, oak-and-maple woodland, and open prairie. The dunes show a fascinating progression from younger dunes nearest the lake that are bare of vegetation or are covered with grasses, to older dunes farther inland that are covered with deciduous woodland. More than 1,400 varieties of trees, shrubs, wildflowers, and other flora have been identified in the national lakeshore—a remarkably high figure for such a relatively small area. At least 270 species of birds have been recorded in the area. Swimming is, of course, a very popular form of recreation during the warmer months. Many hiking trails, a bicycling trail, and interpretive programs help visitors to experience, enjoy, and learn about this amazing place that was saved from industrial or other commercial development. The national lakeshore was established in 1966. Indiana Dunes State Park is located within the boundaries of the national lakeshore and also provides trails, a nature center, and other facilities.

OUTSTANDING FEATURES

Among the many outstanding features of the park are the following: **Mount Baldy**, a moving sand dune at the east end of the lakeshore, the appearance of which changes daily; also notable for the unusual "singing sands" sound caused by the combination of quartz crystals, moisture, pressure, and friction when a person walks on the sand; **Bailly Homestead**, an 1822 trading post and home of fur trader Joseph Bailly and his family; **Chellberg Farm**, a site established in 1872 by Swedish immigrants Anders and Johanna Chellberg and occupied by three generations of Chellbergs, who raised such crops as corn, wheat, oats, rye, garden vegetables, and orchard fruits; and **Pinhook Bog**, an ecologically rich wetlands environment in a low area, which was created when a huge chunk of ice was marooned by the retreating mass of the continental glacier 14,000 years ago and now is filled with pitcher plants, sundews, sphagnum moss, and other interesting plantlife.

PRACTICAL INFORMATION

When to Go

The national lakeshore is open year-round. Summer is the most popular, when temperatures reach into the 80s and 90s in July and August. Other than the unusual subzero cold snap, winter temperatures are typically in the 20s and 30s. Spring weather is variable—wet and cool or warm and balmy, but a time when the landscape is rich with wildflowers. Autumn often offers beautiful weather with clear skies, comfortable temperatures, and colorful foliage.

How to Get There

By Car: U.S. Route 12 runs east-west through the length of the national lakeshore between Michigan City and Gary.

By Air: O'Hare International, Midway, and South Bend airports are served by most major airlines.

By Train: Amtrak (800-872-7245) has stops in Hammond-Whiting. The South Shore Railroad (800-356-2079) from Chicago or South Bend has stops in Miller, Ogden Dunes, Dune Park, and Beverly Shores.

By Bus: Greyhound Lines (800-231-2222) has stops in Michigan City and Gary, Indiana.

Fees and Permits

No entrance fees are charged. A state fishing license and trout-salmon stamps are required to fish; they can be purchased locally. A one-day, nonresident fishing license is available. Parking at West Beach is $3.00 per vehicle from May through September. Fees at Dunewood Campground are $10 per night for a regular site and $8 per night for a walk-in site.

Visitor Center, Education Center, and Contact Stations

Dorothy Buell Memorial Visitor Center, three miles east of State Route 49 on U.S. Route 12: open daily, except on Thanksgiving, Christmas, and New Year's Day. Activity schedules, information, interpretive exhibits, video program, and publications. A nearby trail in an area of scenic wooded dunes is handicapped-accessible.

Paul H. Douglas Center for Environmental Education: open Monday through Friday, closed weekends and holidays. Environmental studies for adults and children and interpretive exhibits. For more information, call 219-938-8221.

Bailly-Chellberg Visitor Contact Station: Interpretive exhibits, information, and publications. Late 19th- and early 20th-century farming demonstrations at Chellberg Farm and early 19th-century fur-trading demonstrations at Bailly Homestead are presented throughout the year. "Maple Sugar Time" program is held in mid-March, and "Duneland Harvest Festival" is presented on the third weekend of September.

West Beach Visitor Contact Station: open weekends in April and May and in September and October. Interpretive exhibits and information. This 3.5-mile beach also has a bathhouse, picnic area, and trails.

Indiana Dunes State Park's Nature Center: open daily from Memorial Day through Labor Day and weekends year-round. Information, interpretive exhibits, library, children's activities corner, and bird observation room. For more information, call 219-926-1390.

Facilities

Available are bathhouses, picnic areas, campground, and food concessions.

Handicapped Accessibility

Paul H. Douglas Center for Environmental Education, West Beach, Porter Beach, Lake View, Dorothy Buell Memorial Visitor Center, Dunewood Campground, amphitheater and all parking lots, restrooms, and fountains are wheelchair-accessible. Also accessible are trails in ten out of 13 areas and seven picnic areas. On West Beach, a sand/snow chair is available throughout the year. Telecommunications Devices for the Deaf (TDD) are available at the visitor center, the environmental education center, park headquarters, and ranger stations. The slide program at the visitor center is captioned, and tactile interpretive exhibits are provided. A folder providing information on handicapped access to the lakeshore is available on request.

Medical Services

First aid is available at the West Beach bathhouse (summer only) and Bailly Ranger Station. The closest hospitals are in Michigan City, Gary, and Valparaiso.

Pets

Pets are not allowed in swimming areas and must be leashed or otherwise physically restrained at all times. Leashes may not exceed six feet.

Safety and Regulations

For your safety and enjoyment and for the protection of the park, please follow these regulations and suggestions:

- Remember that plants, animals, and natural and historic features are protected by law, so visitors are urged not to disturb, damage, or destroy them.

- As some areas within the national lakeshore are privately owned, please respect private properties and do not trespass.

- Public hunting and trapping are prohibited.

- Ground fires are not permitted. Instead, use fire grates, grills, or portable charcoal, gas, or liquid fuel stoves.

- Hang gliding may be pursued at Mount Baldy only by permit.

- Bicycling is allowed only on designated trails.
- Boaters must stay 500 feet from marked swimming areas.
- Lake Michigan waters can be hazardous, and rip currents frequently occur during periods of high wind and waves.
- In winter, shelf ice often forms along the lakeshore and is never safe to walk on.
- Be sure to protect yourself from sun, poison ivy, ticks, mosquitoes, and other biting insects. To report emergencies and accidents, call 219-926-1952 or 800-PARK-TIP.

ACTIVITIES

Options include swimming, hiking, birdwatching, boating, bicycling, horseback riding, picnicking, camping, fishing, cross-country skiing, snow-shoeing, environmental education and interpretive programs, and special festivals and other events. Further details regarding activities and events are available in the national lakeshore's newspaper, *Singing Sands Almanac*.

Hiking Trails

Among the many trails are the following: **Calumet Dune Trail**, an easy, .8-mile, self-guided interpretive paved trail beginning at the Dorothy Buell Memorial Visitor Center and following Calumet Dune Ridge; **Ly-Co-Ki-We Trail** (Ly-co-ki-we is a Miami Indian word meaning "sandy ground"), a moderate, 6.4-mile series of loops beginning at the Dorothy Buell Memorial Visitor Center and crossing two ancient dune ridges, between which is an area of wetland; horseback riding is permitted on this trail from mid-March to mid-December, and in winter cross-country skiing is popular here; extensions of this trail are the 1.8-mile Dunewood Trace, east from the visitor center to Dunewood Campground, and the 1.2-mile Ly-Co-Ki-We Extension running west to the Dune Park Train Station; **Bailly Homestead and Chellberg Farm Trail**, two moderately easy, 1.2-mile or two-mile, self-guided interpretive loops beginning and ending at the Bailly-Chellberg Visitor Contact Station;

Cowles Bog Trail, a moderate-to-strenuous five miles of three loop trails beginning at Dune Acres Entrance Station (north of the Chellberg Farm area) and winding through this ecologically rich area of interdunal ponds, bogs, a stand of white pines, forested dunes, fore-dunes, and beach; **West Beach Trail**, an easy-to-moderate, 2.5-mile, self-guided interpretive route in two loops, with the one-mile Dune Succession Trail beginning on the beach and passing through a variety of habitats, including marram grass (the roots systems of which help to build and stabilize sand dunes), an intradunal pond, an area of jack pines, and a wooded dune with black oaks, hickories, ashes, and basswood; and **Pinhook Bog**, an easy, .75-mile route through Indiana's only real bog, which is accessible only on ranger-led tours available on summer Saturdays and Sundays; for reservations, call 219-926-7561, ext. 225. Indiana Dunes State Park also provides a network of trails.

OVERNIGHT STAYS

Lodging and Dining

No lodging or dining facilities are provided within the national lakeshore boundaries. Accommodations, restaurants, and other businesses are available in such nearby communities as Michigan City, Pines, Chesterton, Porter, and Gary. In the summer months, food concessions are available at West Beach and Mount Baldy.

Campgrounds

Dunewood Campground has both drive-in and walk-in sites. The campground does not take reservations and has no electrical hookups. Indiana Dunes State Park, which is within the boundaries of the national lakeshore, has a campground that accepts reservations; call 219-926-1952.

FLORA AND FAUNA (Partial Listings)

Mammals: whitetail deer, coyote, red and gray foxes, woodchuck, beaver, muskrat, opossum, raccoon, striped skunk, longtail weasel, southern bog lemming, red and gray squirrels, and eastern chipmunk.

Birds: common loon, pied-billed and horned grebes, double-crested cormorant, least bittern, great blue and green-backed herons, Canada goose, wood and black ducks, mallard, blue-winged teal, gadwall, wigeon, redhead, ring-necked duck, common goldeneye, bufflehead, red-breasted merganser, turkey vulture, hawks (sharp-shinned, red-shouldered, broad-winged, and red-tailed), kestrel, bobwhite, Virginia and sora rails, coot, sandhill crane, killdeer, sandpipers (solitary, spotted, and semipalmated), sanderling, dunlin, woodcock, gulls (Bonaparte's, ring-billed, and herring), Caspian and Forster's terns, mourning dove, owls (screech, great horned, and barred), chimney swift, ruby-throated hummingbird, belted kingfisher, woodpeckers (red-headed, red-bellied, downy, hairy, and pileated), flicker, eastern wood pewee, flycatchers (Acadian, willow, least, and great crested), eastern phoebe, eastern kingbird, purple martin, swallows (tree, bank, and barn), blue jay, crow, black-capped chickadee, tufted titmouse, white-breasted nuthatch, brown creeper, wrens (Carolina, house, and marsh), golden-crowned and ruby-crowned kinglets, blue-gray gnatcatcher, eastern bluebird, veery, thrushes (Swainson's, hermit, and wood), robin, catbird, brown thrasher, vireos (yellow-throated, warbling, and red-eyed), warblers (blue-winged, yellow-winged, Tennessee, Nashville, yellow, chestnut-sided, magnolia, Cape May, yellow-rumped, black-throated green, blackburnian, prairie, palm, bay-breasted, blackpoll, cerulean, black-and-white, prothonotary, mourning, Wilson's, and Canada), American redstart, ovenbird, northern waterthrush, common yellowthroat, yellow-breasted chat, scarlet tanager, cardinal, rose-breasted grosbeak, indigo bunting, rufous-sided towhee, sparrows (tree, chipping, field, vesper, savannah, fox, song, swamp, and white-throated), dark-eyed junco, bobolink, red-winged blackbird, eastern meadowlark, common grackle, Baltimore oriole, purple finch, house finch, and American goldfinch.

Trees, Shrubs, and Flowers: white and jack pines, common juniper, tulip tree (yellow poplar), sassafras, witch hazel, white and black oaks, American basswood, eastern cottonwood, black cherry, flowering dogwood, sugar maple, arctic bearberry, arrowhead, asters, beach pea, bell flower, bloodroot, Canada mayflower, cardinal flower, columbine, Dutchman's breeches, evening primrose, false heather, fireweed, fringed gentian, goldenrods, harebell, hepatica, Indian paintbrush, Indian pipe, iris, Jack-in-the-pulpit, Joe Pye weed, ladies' tresses, lizard's tail, marsh marigold, May apple, northern fringed orchid, phlox, prickly-pear cactus, St. Johnswort, sea rocket, skunk cabbage, spring beauty, starflower, sundew, swamp aster, swamp candle, swamp loosestrife, swamp rose, trillium, trout lily, violet, water lily, wild ginger, and yellow lady-slipper.

NEARBY POINTS OF INTEREST

The area surrounding Indiana Dunes National Lakeshore offers other interesting attractions that can be enjoyed as day trips or overnight excursions. The Calumet Prairie and Hoosier Prairie state nature preserves are located nearby. The Chicago Portage National Historic Site is on the western shores of the lake in Chicago, and the Illinois and Michigan Canal National Heritage Corridor is to the southwest.

Isle Royale National Park

▲ *Rock Harbor Light*

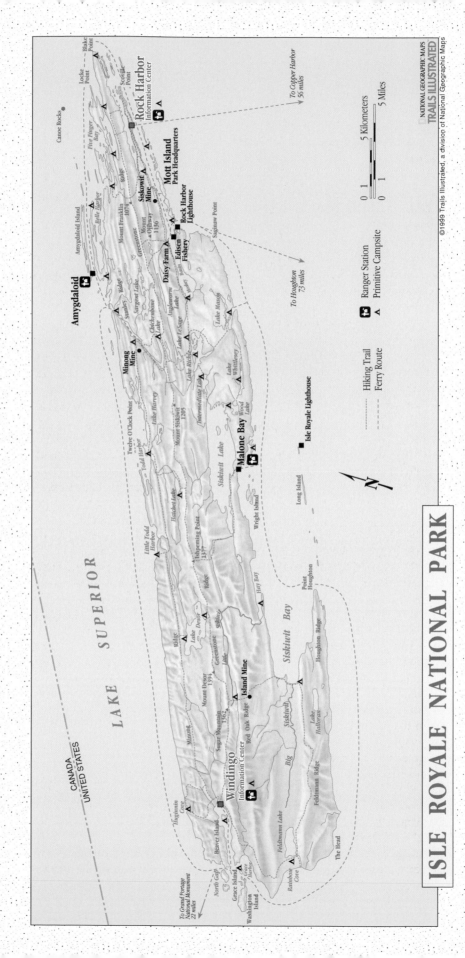

ISLE ROYALE NATIONAL PARK

LAKE SUPERIOR

CANADA
UNITED STATES

Canoe Rocks

Blake Point
Locke Point
Scoville Point
Rock Harbor
Information Center

To Copper Harbor
56 miles

Five Finger Bay

Amygdaloid Island
Belle Harbor
Ridge

Mott Island
Park Headquarters

Mount Franklin 1074
Greenstone
Mount Ojibway 1136
Siskowit Mine

Rock Harbor Lighthouse

Amygdaloid

Daisy Farm
Edisen Fishery

Saginaw Point

Stanley Ridge
Sargent Lake
Chickenbone Lake
Minong Mine
Lake LeSage
Lake Richie
Inglalston Lake
Lake Mason

To Houghton
73 miles

Twelve O'Clock Point
Todd Harbor
Lake Harvey
Mount Siskiwit
Intermediate Lake
Lake Whittlesey
Lake Mason
Wood Lake

Little Todd Harbor
Hatchet Lake
Ishpeming Point 1377
Siskiwit Lake
Malone Bay
Isle Royale Lighthouse

Long Island

Hay Bay
Wright Island

Ridge
Lake Desor
Greenstone Ridge
Siskiwit

Point Houghton

Ridge
Mount Desor 1394
Mount Siskiwit

Minong
Sugar Mountain 1362
Island Mine
Red Oak Ridge

Houghton Ridge

Siskiwit Bay

Windingo
Information Center

Big
Siskiwit

Lake
Halloran

Feldtmann Ridge

Tinguuin Cove
Beaver Island
Feldtmann Lake

The Head

To Grand Portage
National Monument
22 miles

North Gap
Grace Harbor
Grace Island
Washington Island
Rainbow Cove

Ranger Station
Primitive Campsite

Hiking Trail
Ferry Route

0   1   5 Kilometers
0   1   5 Miles

NATIONAL GEOGRAPHIC MAPS
TRAILS ILLUSTRATED
©1999 Trails Illustrated, a division of National Geographic Maps

Isle Royale National Park

**800 East Lakeshore Drive
Houghton, MI 49931-1895
906-482-0984**

This 571,790-acre national park protects a magnificent wilderness archipelago and surrounding waters in northwest Lake Superior. The roadless park's main feature is Isle Royale, which measures nearly 40 miles long and nine miles at its widest, with elevations ranging from 600 feet above sea level along Lake Superior to 1,394 feet atop Mount Desor. The island contains a multitude of exquisitely beautiful bays, harbors, coves, and peninsulas; 50 sparkling lakes; numerous rivers and streams; bogs, marshes, and cedar swamps; long, glacier-sculpted ridges; many smaller off-shore islands, some forming chains of long, narrow little islets; a forest that is an ecologically rich mixture of coniferous and deciduous trees; and a diversity of wildlife, highlighted by the gray wolf and moose. More than 200 species of birds have been recorded in the park, along with approximately 700 varieties of plantlife.

Since 1958, wolf-moose, predator-prey interrelationships, population fluctuations, and their impact upon the environment on Isle Royale have been the subject of intense research. The wolf population has been of particular recent concern, since according to the *Ecological Studies of Wolves on Isle Royale, 1997-1998*, "After several years of steady population increase, wolves unexpectedly declined to just 14 individuals in 1998, down from 24 in 1997." That document goes on to report that "acute food shortage arising from the moose die-off [273] in 1996 is a likely cause of the wolf decline" and that "mortality in the past year was the highest ever observed for this population." An estimated 700 moose were recorded during this study period, down from around 2,400 in 1995.

The park was authorized in 1931 and was established in 1940. Part of the area was designated as wilderness in 1976, and it was named as a Biosphere Reserve in 1980.

OUTSTANDING FEATURES

Among the many outstanding features of the park are the following: **Rock Harbor**, a long, narrow waterway that is the primary access to the eastern end of the island, reached by boat from Houghton and Copper Harbor, Michigan; **Washington Harbor**, a fjord-like waterway that is the main access to the western end of the island at Windigo; **Scoville Point**, an area east of Rock Harbor that affords a view of rocky islets at the east end of Isle Royale; **Suzy's Cave**, a natural arch sculpted by water near the Rock Harbor Trail; **Lookout Louise**, a 320-foot summit above Lake Superior, offering a wonderful view of bays, coves, and islands along the northeastern shore of Isle Royale; **Mount Ojibway**, at 1,136 feet above sea level and topped with a lookout tower, the highest summit on the eastern end of Isle Royale; **Ishpeming Point**, at 1,377 feet and topped with a lookout tower, the second highest summit on the island; **Mount Desor**, at 1,394 feet elevation, the highest point in the park; **Siskiwit Lake**, the largest lake on Isle Royale; **Raspberry Island**, a long, narrow island near Rock Harbor that is covered with a boreal forest and contains a bog; **Edisen Fishery**, a group of restored historic cabins and other structures once owned by Pete Edisen, one of the last commercial fisherman on the island; **Rock Harbor Lighthouse**, a structure dating from 1855 and located a short walk from Edisen Fishery; and **Minong Mine**, the site (near McCargoe Cove on the island's northern shore) of Minong Mining Company's long-abandoned, 19th-century, copper-ore exploration and mining activities— once the largest of many scattered across the island.

PRACTICAL INFORMATION

When to Go

The park is open from mid-April through October, and full visitor services are provided only from mid-June through Labor Day. In spring, dense fog and thunderstorms are common. Summer temperatures rarely exceed 80 degrees, and evenings can be quite cool. Blueberries ripen in late July and August. Autumn foliage is beautiful, especially between mid-September and mid-October.

How to Get There

By Car: In Michigan's Upper Peninsula, from State Route 28, drive north onto the Keweenaw Peninsula, by either U.S. Route 41 or U.S. Route 45 and State Route 26, to Houghton for boat service to Isle Royale; or continuing on through Houghton on U.S. Route 41, drive to Copper Harbor for boat service to the park. From Duluth, Minnesota, drive northeast 145 miles on State Route 61 to Grand Portage National Monument for boat service to Isle Royale.

By Air: From airports in Houghton, Michigan, and Duluth, Minnesota, float-planes can be chartered daily except Sundays from late-May through late-September. Contact Isle Royale Seaplane Service, P.O. Box 366, Houghton, MI 49931; 906-482-8850.

By Train: Amtrak (800-872-7245) has stops in Minneapolis.

By Boat: There are four options. The *Isle Royale Queen III* makes the 4.5-hour trip from Copper Harbor to Rock Harbor from mid-June through September. The service is available daily in August; in other months, there is no service on some days of the week. Reservations, which are advised far in advance, may be made by contacting The Royale Line, Box 24, Copper Harbor, MI 49918; 906-289-4437.

The *Ranger III* makes the 6.5-hour trip from Houghton to Rock Harbor from June through early September two days per week in each direction. Reservations, which are advised far in advance, may be made by contacting Isle Royale National Park, 800 E. Lakeshore Dr., Houghton, MI 49931; 906-482-8753.

The *Voyageur II* makes the two-hour trip from Grand Portage to Windigo or the seven-hour trip from Grand Portage to Rock Harbor from early May through late October on certain days of the week. The *Wenonah* makes the

three-hour trip from Grand Portage to Windigo daily. Reservations are advised far in advance. GP-IR Transportation Line, Inc., 1507 N. First St., Superior, WI 54880, 715-392-2100, handles boat service from Grand Portage to Windigo, Rock Harbor, and areas in between.

Fees and Permits

No entrance fees are charged, but fees are charged for access to the park by boat and for other boat trips. Permits, available at park information centers at Rock Harbor and Windigo, are required for camping, boating, and scuba diving.

Visitor Center and Information Centers

Houghton Visitor Center, at park headquarters in Houghton, Michigan: Park information, publications, maps, and permits.

Rock Harbor Information Center: open daily during the season. Park information, publications, maps, and permits.

Windigo Information Center: open daily during the season. Park information, publications, maps, and permits.

Facilities

Available are a marina with fuel and pump-out stations, three-sided shelters, hot showers, laundry, lodging, restaurant, and snack bar.

Handicapped Accessibility

Park headquarters in Houghton, information centers, Rock Harbor Lodge, and a campsite at Daisy Farm are wheelchair-accessible. Access to boats requires assistance. Detailed information is available by contacting the park.

Medical Services

Medical services are not available in the park, other than first aid, which is available at ranger stations and information centers. Seriously ill or injured persons are transported to the mainland at their own expense. Campers, hikers, and boaters should carry a well-equipped first-aid kit and be prepared to handle their own emergencies. The nearest hospital is in Houghton.

Pets

Pets are not permitted within the park, even if they are kept aboard vessels. (Special conditions apply to guide and service dogs.)

Safety and Regulations

For your safety and enjoyment and for the protection of the park, please follow these regulations and suggestions:

- No public telephone service is available; emergency messages only can be sent through the park's radio system.

- Mosquitoes, gnats, and black flies are abundant, especially early in the season, so visitors are advised to bring insect repellent, and campers should be equipped with netting.

- Remember that it is unlawful to feed, disturb, or kill wildlife.

- Firearms are not permitted in the park.

- Personal items, food, or packs should not be left unattended.

- Visitors are forewarned that inclement weather and rough water may delay departures up to several days.

- Swimmers are warned that the waters of Lake Superior are very cold and that leeches inhabit the shallow inland lakes of Isle Royale.

- All surface water in the park may be considered contaminated with the eggs of the hydatid tapeworm and bacteria. Consequently, all water should be filtered or boiled for at least two minutes.

- U.S. citizens returning from Canada and Canadian visitors to the island must clear U.S. Customs. A U.S. Customs and Immigration Officer is usually available during normal working hours at Rock Harbor, Windigo, and Amygdaloid ranger stations.

ACTIVITIES

Options include boating, canoeing, kayaking, boat cruises, canoe tours, boat tours, boat rentals, canoe rentals, motor rentals, water taxi service, hiking and portaging trails, guided fishing trips, scuba diving, birdwatching, nature and history walks and talks, lighthouse and copper mine tours, interpretive films, evening programs, camping, and fishing. Further information is provided in the park's newspaper, *The Greenstone*.

Hiking Trails

The more than 160 miles of trails on the island include the following:

Originating at Rock Harbor Lodge: **Kneutson Trail**, an easy quarter-mile, self-guided interpretive route, tracing the history of this part of Isle Royale; and **Scoville Point (Stoll) Trail**, a fairly easy, four-mile loop through spruce-fir forest and bog habitats, with a 1.5-mile spur along the rocky end of Scoville Point. Along the loop trail are shallow mining pits, where outcrops of copper nuggets and veins were removed by pre-Columbian miners from roughly 2500 B.C. to 1000 B.C. More than a thousand such pits at seven places have been found on Isle Royale, from which an estimated 300 tons of this remarkably pure form of copper were extracted. The metal was traded among early Indian tribes throughout much of this region of North America and crafted into knives, fishhooks, pendants, and beads.

On Raspberry Island: **Raspberry Island Trail**, an easy, one-mile loop beginning at the boat dock and leading through a bog with black spruces, pitcher plants, and sundews and past shore cliffs.

In the Rock Harbor Lighthouse vicinity: **Edisen Fishery-Rock Harbor Lighthouse Trail**, an easy half-mile loop beginning at the boat dock (seven-mile boat tour from Rock Harbor Lodge) and connecting the historic fishery with the lighthouse. Both the fishery and lighthouse offer interpretive exhibits.

In the Malone Bay vicinity: **Siskiwit Lake Trail**, an easy half-mile route from Malone Bay boat dock along a stream to the island's largest lake.

In the McCargoe Cove vicinity: **Minong Mine Trail**, a moderate, one-mile route beginning at the McCargoe Cove boat dock

▲ *Lichen-covered rocks, Isle Royale National Park, Michigan*

and the historic Minong Mine Company town site, to ridge-top pre-Columbian and historic copper mining pits.

In the Windigo vicinity: **Huginnin Trail**, a moderately strenuous, 9.5-mile loop trail beginning and ending at Windigo, passing the ancient Windigo Mines site, and reaching beautiful Huginnin Cove where a campsite is located on Isle Royale's north shore; and **Feldtmann Trail**, a fairly strenuous, 24-mile loop trail (requiring at least three nights at campsites), beginning and ending at Windigo, climbing and providing outstanding panoramas from the escarpment of Feldtmann Ridge, reaching the shore of Siskiwit Bay, and running along Greenstone Ridge.

Between Windigo and Rock Harbor: **Greenstone Ridge Trail**, a fairly strenuous, 40-mile route running along the spine of Isle Royale, between Windigo and Lookout Louise and down to Rock Harbor (requiring at least five days). Variations of this route descend from either Mount Ojibway or Mount Franklin to the Rock Harbor shore trail.

Canoe Portages: The park offers 16 canoe portages, including the following in the Siskiwit Lake vicinity: **Malone Bay-Siskiwit Lake**, a .3-mile, 40-foot gradual climb; **Siskiwit Lake-Intermediate Lake**, a .4-mile, 40-foot, gradual climb; **Intermediate Lake-Lake Richie**, a .6-mile, 120-foot hilly climb; **Wood Lake-Lake Whittlesey**, a .6-mile, 80-foot climb. Among the portages between coves and bays are: **Rock Harbor-Tobin Harbor**, a .2-mile, 40-foot climb up and over; **Five-Finger Bay-Duncan Bay**, a .2-mile, 8-foot climb up and over; and **Pickerel Cove**: a .1-mile, ten-foot climb up and over.

OVERNIGHT STAYS

Lodging and Dining

Rock Harbor Lodge, a popular resort dating from the early 20th century that was sold to the federal government in 1938, provides rooms, housekeeping cabins, dining room, snack bar, gift shop, camping supplies store, and marina. Open during the park's operating season. For reservations, which are advised far in advance, contact National Park Concessions, Inc., at their summer address at P.O. Box 605, Houghton, MI 49931; 906-337-4993, or their winter address at P.O. Box 27, Mammoth Cave, KY 42259; 502-773-2191.

Camping

All camping in the backcountry is on a first-come, first-served basis. A free permit is required and can be obtained at park head-quarters, information centers, and ranger stations. The island has 88 three-sided sleeping shelters with screened fronts that are available on a first-come, first-served basis. Tent sites (for a maximum of six people and three tents) and group sites (for seven to ten people) are also available. Contact the park for specific group camping information. Some sites are accessible through a combination of canoeing and portaging, and docks are available at all boat-in sites.

Campers need to bring a self-contained fuel stove because open wood fires are prohibited in most campgrounds and should consider carrying a water filter capable of filtering to 0.4 microns. The National Park Service urges campers not to bury, burn, or scatter trash but to "pack out everything." An appropriate slogan for helping to protect the fragile environment of this island park is to "leave only footprints."

FLORA AND FAUNA (Partial Listings)

Mammals: moose, gray wolf, red fox, mink, river otter, shorttail weasel, beaver, muskrat, snowshoe hare, red squirrel, and woodland deer mouse.

Birds: common loon, double-crested cormorant, black duck, mallard, common goldeneye, mergansers (common, red-breasted, and hooded), ring-billed and herring gulls, great blue heron, spotted sandpiper, red-tailed and broad-winged hawks, bald eagle, osprey, kestrel, American bittern, great horned and barred owls, belted kingfisher, ruby-throated hummingbird, woodpeckers (pileated, downy, hairy, three-toed, and black-backed), flicker, yellow-bellied sapsucker, eastern kingbird, eastern wood pewee, flycatchers (olive-sided, least, and alder), eastern phoebe, chimney swift, swallows (tree, bank, and barn), raven, blue and gray jays, black-capped and boreal chickadees, red-breasted nuthatch, winter wren, ruby-crowned and golden-crowned kinglets, robin, veery, Swainson's and hermit thrushes, cedar waxwing, solitary and red-eyed vireos, warblers (magnolia, yellow-rumped, Canada, black-throated green, black-throated blue, black-and-white, Cape May, chestnut-sided, bay-breasted, blackburnian, Nashville, Connecticut, mourning, yellow, palm, Tennessee, common yellowthroat, Wilson's, and northern parula), American redstart, ovenbird, northern waterthrush, red-winged blackbird, sparrows (white-throated, chipping, swamp, and song), dark-eyed junco, rose-breasted and evening grosbeaks, red and white-winged crossbills, purple finch, and American goldfinch.

Amphibians and Reptiles: red-spotted newt, mudpuppy and blue-spotted salamanders, spring peeper, frogs (chorus, green, mink, and wood), American toad, western painted turtle, and garter snake.

Trees, Shrubs, and Flowers: pines (white, red, and jack), tamarack (rare), white and black spruces, balsam fir, northern white cedar, northern red oak, yellow and paper birches, balsam poplar, quaking and bigtooth aspens, common chokecherry, American mountain-ash, maples (mountain, red, and sugar), black ash, Labrador tea, blueberry, bearberry, skunk cabbage, common arrowhead, marsh marigold, pussytoes, spreading dogbane, meadow anemone, iris, wild lily-of-the-valley, twinflower, starflower, large white trillium, clintonia, white rattlesnake root, bunchberry, dewberry, pipsissewa, rock clematis, pale corydalis, Bishop's cap, devilsclub, early saxifrage, Labrador Solomon-plume, pearly everlasting, western thimbleberry, sarsaparilla, wood lily, yellow pond lily, pitcher plant, roundleaf sundew, swamp candle, beach pea, shrubby cinquefoil, toadflax, calypso orchid, green and one-sided pyrolas, shinleaf, spurred gentian, Indian pipe, eastern paintbrush, goldenrods, and asters.

NEARBY POINTS OF INTEREST

The area surrounding Isle Royale National Park offers other fascinating natural and historic attractions that can be enjoyed as day trips or overnight excursions. Grand Portage National Monument is just to the west in northeast Minnesota; Apostle Islands National Lakeshore is to the southwest in Wisconsin; Keweenaw National Historical Park and Porcupine Mountains State Park are to the south on Michigan's Upper Peninsula; and Pictured Rocks National Lakeshore is to the southeast on Michigan's Upper Peninsula.

THEODORE ROOSEVELT NATIONAL PARK

▲ *Scenic badlands*

THEODORE ROOSEVELT NATIONAL PARK

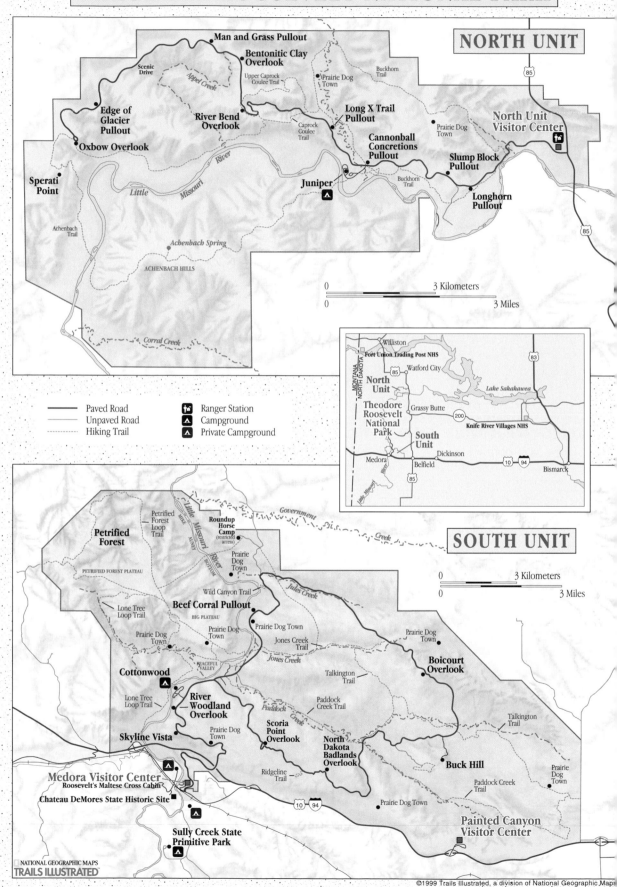

NORTH UNIT

Man and Grass Pullout

Bentonitic Clay Overlook

Scenic Drive

Appel Creek

Upper Caprock Coulee Trail

Prairie Dog Town

Buckhorn Trail

85

Edge of Glacier Pullout

River Bend Overlook

Caprock Coulee Trail

Long X Trail Pullout

North Unit Visitor Center

Oxbow Overlook

Little Missouri River

Cannonball Concretions Pullout

Prairie Dog Town

Slump Block Pullout

Sperati Point

Juniper

Buckhorn Trail

Longhorn Pullout

Achenbach Trail

Achenbach Spring

ACHENBACH HILLS

85

Corral Creek

0   3 Kilometers
0   3 Miles

Williston

Fort Union Trading Post NHS

MONTANA / NORTH DAKOTA

83

Watford City

85

North Unit

Lake Sakakawea

Theodore Roosevelt National Park

Grassy Butte

200

Knife River Villages NHS

South Unit

Medora

Dickinson

Belfield

10   94

Bismarck

85

Paved Road
Unpaved Road
Hiking Trail

Ranger Station
Campground
Private Campground

SOUTH UNIT

Little Missouri River

Government Creek

Petrified Forest Loop Trail

Petrified Forest

Roundup Horse Camp (restricted access)

Prairie Dog Town

PETRIFIED FOREST PLATEAU

Jules Creek

Wild Canyon Trail

Lone Tree Loop Trail

Beef Corral Pullout

BIG PLATEAU

Prairie Dog Town

Prairie Dog Town

Prairie Dog Town

Prairie Dog Town

Boicourt Overlook

Cottonwood

PEACEFUL VALLEY

Jones Creek Trail

Jones Creek

Talkington Trail

Lone Tree Loop Trail

River Woodland Overlook

Prairie Dog Town

Paddock Creek Trail

Paddock Creek

Talkington Trail

Skyline Vista

Scoria Point Overlook

North Dakota Badlands Overlook

Buck Hill

Prairie Dog Town

Medora Visitor Center
Roosevelt's Maltese Cross Cabin

Chateau DeMores State Historic Site

Ridgeline Trail

10   94

Prairie Dog Town

Paddock Creek Trail

Sully Creek State Primitive Park

Painted Canyon Visitor Center

0   3 Kilometers
0   3 Miles

THEODORE ROOSEVELT NATIONAL PARK

P.O. Box 7
Medora, ND 58645-0007
701-623-4466

This three-unit, 70,446-acre national park honors the memory and accomplishments of Theodore Roosevelt, the 26th president of the United States, who drew strength and inspiration from this awesomely scenic, arid, and rugged land in western North Dakota. The park encompasses weather-sculpted badlands, meandering stretches of the Little Missouri River, bordering woodlands, and expanses of shortgrass prairie. These landscapes look much as they did when Roosevelt first came from New York to ride horseback, hunt bison (buffalo), and begin cattle ranching in September 1883.

This challenging environment instilled in "T.R." not only a deep appreciation of this land, but an understanding of the need to protect it and the region's rapidly declining populations of bison and other wildlife. As U.S. president from 1901 to 1909, Roosevelt became an aggressive champion of America's natural resources. Under his pioneering conservation policies, including the Antiquities Act of 1906, many national forests, national parks, and the first few national monuments and national wildlife refuges were established.

Today, visitors have the opportunity to enjoy these landscapes that changed the course of resource conservation history by driving the scenic roads through the North and South units; by hiking the many trails that wind throughout the park; and, in years of adequate precipitation, by canoeing the Little Missouri River (mostly during April, May, and June). The Elkhorn Ranch unit, protecting the site of Roosevelt's principal North Dakota residence, is remote and offers no visitor facilities. The park's abundant wildlife includes herds of bison, pronghorns, bighorn sheep, elk, deer, numerous prairie dog "towns," and more than 200 species of birds. Bands of wild horses roam parts of the park, and a small herd of longhorn cattle can be seen in the North Unit.

Some of the colorfully banded strata of the badlands are relatively soft sandstone and other sedimentary layers, resulting from vast quantities of sand and clay that eroded down from mountains to the west. This erosion occurred 55 million to 60 million years ago during the Paleocene Epoch, when dinosaurs had just become extinct and mammals were evolving toward dominance. Other soft sedimentary layers consist of volcanic ash from numerous, massive volcanic eruptions to the west when what is now arid prairie and badlands was then a lushly forested and swampy environment. From time to time, volcanic ash buried trees and animals. Some of this organic matter, being quickly deprived of oxygen, did not decay, but was transformed and preserved as petrified wood and the fossilized remains of trees (including ancient forms of sequoias and palms), leaf prints, clams, snails, crocodiles, birds, and small mammals. The erosion of the sedimentary layers over the past half-million years or more has carved the land into a badlands topography of intriguing bluffs, mesas, ridges, buttes, domes, knobs, caprocks, pillars, gullies, and gorges. In the process, this erosion has also exposed some of the petrified wood and fossils.

In 1947, Theodore Roosevelt National Memorial Park was established. In 1978, it was renamed a national park and nearly half the area was designated wilderness.

OUTSTANDING FEATURES

Among the many outstanding features of the park are the following: **Painted Canyon Overlook**, a spot just off I-94 (seven miles east of Medora) that provides an excellent view of the South Unit's colorful badlands; **Medora**, a small, historic village at the south entrance to the park, which was founded by a French nobleman; **Maltese Cross Cabin**, a restored log structure (now relocated adjacent to the park's Medora Visitor Center) that was T.R.'s home in 1884-85 and the headquarters of his cattle operations that peaked in 1885-86; **Little Missouri River**, which meanders through the park, its banks shaded along some stretches by cottonwoods and other bottomland trees as viewed from River Woodland Overlook and elsewhere; **Scoria Point**, an overlook in an area containing brightly colored, fire-baked formations of sedimentary rock that provides excellent views of the South Unit's badlands; **Buck Hill**, a small hill, 2,855 feet above sea level, offering a wonderful panorama of the eastern end of the park's South Unit; **Boicourt Overlook**, one of the most impressive views from the loop drive of the South Unit's badlands; **Wind Canyon**, a narrow side canyon in the South Unit near a graceful oxbow in the Little Missouri River, which is being eroded by water and by grains of sand carried from the riverbed by prevailing northwesterly winds; **Caprock Coulee**, a spectacular arrangement of caprock formations reached by trail through badlands coulees (dry gulches) in the park's North Unit; **River Bend Overlook**, a magnificent view of the badlands-bordered Little Missouri River, located in the North Unit; **Oxbow Overlook**, a point at the end of the North Unit's scenic drive that provides one of the most magnificent panoramas of the river; and **Elkhorn Ranch site**, an area within a remote separate unit of the park that was, for several years, Theodore Roosevelt's home ranch and private retreat until the severe winter of 1887, when 60 percent of his cattle perished and his ranching operations sharply declined.

PRACTICAL INFORMATION

When to Go

The park is open year-round although winter weather may necessitate road closings, and services are limited from October to May. Long, warm days with low humidity and cool evenings make summer popular. Winters are especially long, with the first freezing temperatures arriving by October. Wildflowers bloom in late spring and early summer, and trees along the Little Missouri and elsewhere turn yellow and gold in the autumn.

How to Get There

By Car: To reach the South Unit: from Bismarck, North Dakota, drive west 135 miles on I-94 and exit at Medora; or from Glendive, Montana, drive east 60 miles on I-94 and exit

at Medora. To reach the North Unit: from I-94 at Belfield, drive north about 19 miles on U.S. Route 85.

By Air: Bismarck Municipal Airport (701-222-6502) is the closest major airport. Dickinson Airport has limited connections via smaller commuter aircraft.

By Train: Amtrak (800-872-7245) has stops in Williston, north of the park.

By Bus: Greyhound Lines (800-231-2222) has stops in Medora and Belfield.

Fees and Permits

Entrance fees, collected from May to September, are $10 per vehicle or $5 per person. A free permit, available at visitor centers, is required for backcountry camping. A state fishing license is also required.

Visitor Centers

Medora Visitor Center, in the South Unit: open daily, except Thanksgiving, Christmas, and New Year's Day. Interpretive exhibits that include some personal items of Theodore Roosevelt and ranching artifacts, audiovisual programs, publications, maps, and backcountry permits for the South Unit.

Painted Canyon Visitor Center, in the South Unit seven miles east of Medora: open daily, usually from April through October. Information, publications, and maps.

North Unit Visitor Center: open daily, except Thanksgiving, Christmas, New Year's Day, and occasionally during weekdays in winter. Interpretive exhibits, publications, maps, and backcountry permits for the North Unit.

Facilities

Available are wayside interpretive exhibits along the two scenic drives, trails, picnic areas, and campgrounds.

Handicapped Accessibility

Visitor centers, campgrounds, Maltese Cross Cabin, ranger programs, picnic areas, wayside exhibits, and restrooms are wheelchair-accessible. A detailed guide is available at visitor centers.

Medical Services

First aid is available at the visitor centers. The closest hospitals are in Dickinson, 35 miles from the South Unit, and in Watford City, 15 miles from the North Unit.

Pets

Pets are permitted on leashes that are no more than six feet long, but are prohibited in public buildings and the backcountry and on trails. Horses are prohibited in campgrounds, picnic areas, and on self-guided nature trails.

Safety and Regulations

For your safety and enjoyment and for the protection of the park, please follow these regulations and suggestions:

- The National Park Service warns visitors to view animals, especially bison, from a safe distance. Remember that feeding, disturbing, capturing, and hunting wildlife, as well as damaging or removing plantlife, petrified wood, fossils, and other natural or cultural objects, are prohibited.

- Visitors should be alert for rattlesnakes, black widow spiders, ticks, and poison ivy.

- Bicycles and motor vehicles must stay on established roads.

- Be prepared for sudden weather changes and harsh conditions, such as thunderstorms.

- At campgrounds and picnic areas, fires are allowed only in grates provided or in camp stoves.

- Water in the backcountry is not recommended for human consumption.

The National Park Service asks that visitors not litter the park. Remember the excellent slogan to "leave only footprints" as a guide to help protect this national park.

ACTIVITIES

Options include hiking, horseback riding, bird-watching, interpretive walks and talks, river float trips and canoeing (mostly from April through June), picnicking, camping, and cross-country skiing.

Hiking Trails

Among the many trails in the park are the following:

In the South Unit: **Painted Canyon Overlook Nature Trail**, a fairly easy, .9-mile, self-guided interpretive loop just off I-94 (seven miles east of Medora), providing some outstanding badlands views; **Ridgeline Nature Trail**, an easy .6-mile, self-guided interpretive loop beginning on the loop drive and affording good views of the badlands; **Coal Vein Trail**, an easy .8-mile route where, from 1951 to 1977, a fire burned within a lignite coal seam and baked adjacent sand and clay; **Buck Hill Trail**, a fairly easy, short walk to the summit of this small hill, affording an impressive panorama; **Wind Canyon Nature Trail**, a short, fairly easy climb to see both this small, sand- and water-sculpted canyon and a beautiful bend of the Little Missouri River; **Jones Creek Trail**, a moderately strenuous, 3.7-mile route between two points on the loop drive, following Jones Creek (an intermittent stream) and offering a great opportunity to see the rugged heart of the badlands; **Lower Paddock Creek Trail**, a moderately strenuous, 4.4-mile route between the site of Halliday Well and the loop drive, following Paddock Creek (an intermittent stream) and offering another great opportunity to see the rugged heart of the badlands; **Upper Paddock Creek Trail**, a moderately strenuous, 6.4-mile route, between the loop drive and Southeast Corner Spring, providing a great view of colorful Painted Canyon; and **Petrified Forest Trail**, a fairly strenuous, 16-mile, two- to three-day loop, beginning and ending at Peaceful Valley, leading through the wilderness of the western end of the park's South Unit, and affording views of petrified wood.

In the North Unit: **Little Mo Trail**, an easy, 1.1-mile, self-guided interpretive route beginning at Juniper Campground and leading through an area of scenic woodland and badlands; **Caprock Coulee Nature Trail**, an easy .8-mile, self-guided interpretive loop beginning on the scenic drive (at about 1.5 miles northwest of Juniper

Campground) and leading through badlands coulees (dry gulches) and breaks (interruptions in the plains); and **Upper Caprock Coulee Trail**, a moderate, 4.1-mile loop beginning at the trailhead of the nature trail and including a view of the Little Missouri from the historic River Bend Overlook Shelter, built by the Civilian Conservation Corps, in the 1930s.

Longer routes include the 11-mile Buckhorn and 16-mile Achenbach trails. Most ambitious is the Maah Daah Hey Trail—a 120-mile route for hiking, horseback riding, and mountain biking that is still under construction but when finished will wind through the Little Missouri National Grasslands, state and private lands, and the North and South units of this national park.

OVERNIGHT STAYS

▲ *Bison grazing in the North Unit of Theodore Roosevelt National Park, North Dakota*

Lodging and Dining

No lodging or dining facilities are available within the park. Accommodations are available in such communities as Medora (limited in winter), Belfield, and Beach, along I-94, and in Watford City near the North Unit.

Campgrounds

Sites at Cottonwood Campground in the South Unit and Juniper Campground in the North Unit are available year-round on a first-come, first-served basis. Both campgrounds may occasionally be full during mid-summer.

Camping for groups of eight or more persons requires reservations, which can be made by contacting park headquarters. Campers are advised to bring their own firewood, charcoal, or stove since firewood is not available and wood gathering is not permitted.

Backcountry Camping

Backcountry camping, for which free permits are required, is allowed year-round throughout much of the park on a first-come, first-served basis. There are no designated backcountry sites or facilities.

FLORA AND FAUNA (Partial Listings)

Mammals: bison, bighorn sheep, elk, pronghorn, mule and whitetail deer, mountain lion (rarely), bobcat, coyote, red fox, badger, mink, longtail weasel, beaver, porcupine, raccoon, striped skunk, snowshoe hare, whitetail jackrabbit, desert and eastern cottontails, blacktail prairie dog, red and fox squirrels, thirteen-lined ground squirrel, least chipmunk, and kangaroo rat. The introduced small bands of wild horses and a small herd of longhorn cattle are what the National Park Service calls "historic demonstrations."

Birds: Canada goose, mallard, green-winged teal, white pelican, great blue heron, wild turkey (introduced species), sharp-tailed grouse, killdeer, spotted sandpiper, northern harrier, hawks (sharp-shinned, Cooper's, Swainson's, and red-tailed), golden and bald eagles, kestrel, turkey vulture, owls (great horned, eastern screech, and burrowing), mourning dove, woodpeckers (red-headed, downy, and hairy), flicker, eastern and western kingbirds, least flycatcher, horned lark, chimney swift, swallows (bank, cliff, and barn), crow, black-billed magpie, house and rock wrens, robin, Townsend's solitaire, eastern and mountain bluebirds, loggerhead and northern shrikes, cedar and Bohemian waxwings, warbling and red-eyed vireos, yellow warbler, common yellowthroat, American redstart, yellow-breasted chat, red-winged blackbird, western meadowlark, Bullock's oriole, sparrows (lark, chipping, tree, field, clay-colored,

grasshopper, song, vesper, and savannah), chestnut-collared longspur, spotted towhee, snow bunting, black-headed and evening grosbeaks, lazuli bunting, common redpoll, American goldfinch, pine siskin, and lark bunting.

Amphibians and Reptiles: tiger salamander, leopard and boreal chorus frogs, plains spadefoot and Great Plains toads, turtles (western painted, common snapping, and soft-shelled), sagebrush and short-horned lizards, western plains and red-sided garter snakes, western smooth green snake, plains hognose snake, yellow-bellied racer, bullsnake, and prairie rattlesnake.

Trees, Shrubs, Flowers, and Grasses: junipers (Rocky Mountain, common, and creeping), American elm, eastern cottonwood, sandbar willow, common chokecherry, boxelder, green ash, fragrant sumac (skunkbush), golden currant, buffaloberry, Juneberry, wild plum, prairie and Wood's roses, wolfberry, rabbitbrush, greasewood, spiny saltbush, sagebrushes (big, fringed, and white), winterfat, snakeweed, shrubby cinquefoil, wild strawberry, silver and fringed sages (salvia), narrowleaf yucca, lilies (gumbo, scoria, sego, and purple), yellow Indian paintbrush, blazingstar (dotted gayfeather), scarlet globemallow, harebell, white beardtongue (penstemon), scarlet gaura, moss phlox, goat's beard, pasqueflower, western wallflower, purple prairie clover, purple locoweed, golden pea, prince's plume, Rocky Mountain bee plant, goldenrods, common and stiff sunflowers, purple and prairie coneflowers, aromatic and golden asters, prairie prickly pear and pincushion cacti, and more than 15 species of grasses, including blue and sideoats gramas, buffalograss, Canada wild-rye, little bluestem, needle-and-thread, big sandgrass, and western wheatgrass.

NEARBY POINTS OF INTEREST

The area surrounding Theodore Roosevelt National Park offers other significant natural and cultural attractions that can be enjoyed as day trips or overnight excursions. Little Missouri National Grasslands are adjacent to

53

▲ *Green ash and badlands, South Unit, Theodore Roosevelt National Park, North Dakota*

the park; Chateau de Mores State Historic Site and Sully Creek State Primitive Park are near Medora; Badlands and Wind Cave national parks, Mount Rushmore National Memorial, and Jewel Cave National Monument are to the south in the Black Hills area of South Dakota; Devils Tower National Monument is to the southwest in Wyoming; Fort Union Trading Post National Historic Site and Fort Buford State Historic Site are to the northwest in North Dakota; Medicine Lake National Wildlife Refuge is to the northwest in Montana; and Knife River Indian Villages National Historic Site is to the east in North Dakota.

VOYAGEURS NATIONAL PARK

▲ *Anderson Bay*

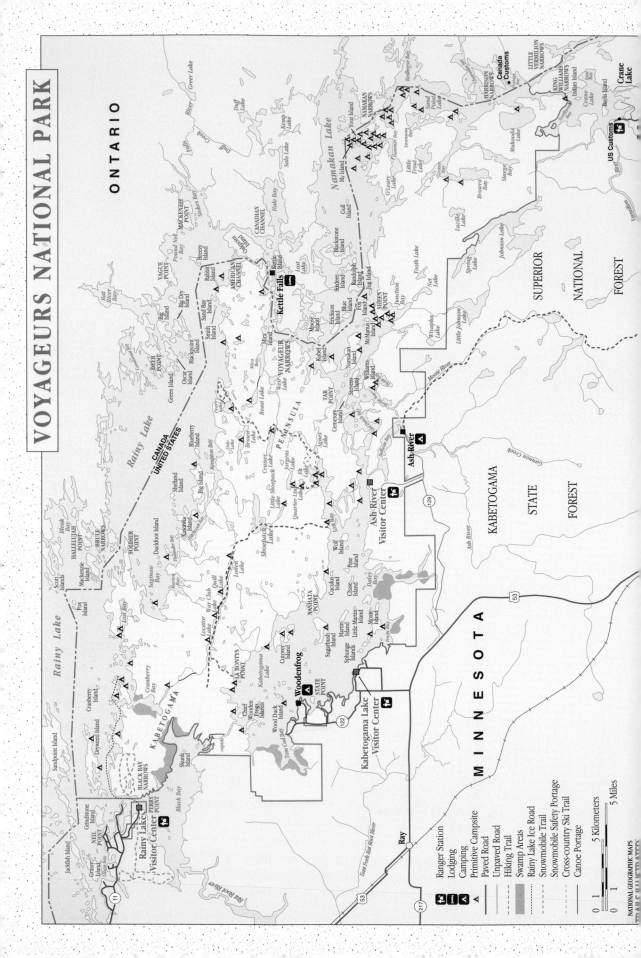

VOYAGEURS NATIONAL PARK

ONTARIO

MINNESOTA

KABETOGAMA STATE FOREST

SUPERIOR NATIONAL FOREST

Rainy Lake

Namakan Lake

KABETOGAMA PENINSULA

Visitor Centers / Points:
Rainy Lake Visitor Center
Kabetogama Lake Visitor Center
Ash River Visitor Center
Woodenfrog
Kettle Falls
Ash River
Crane Lake
Canada Customs
US Customs

NATIONAL GEOGRAPHIC MAPS

Legend:
- Ranger Station
- Lodging
- Camping
- Primitive Campsite
- Paved Road
- Unpaved Road
- Hiking Trail
- Swamp Areas
- Rainy Lake Ice Road
- Snowmobile Trail
- Snowmobile Safety Portage
- Cross-country Ski Trail
- Canoe Portage

0 1 5 Kilometers
0 1 5 Miles

CANADA / UNITED STATES

VOYAGEURS NATIONAL PARK

3131 Highway 53
International Falls, MN 56649-8904
218-283-9821

Established in 1975, this 218,035-acre national park in northern Minnesota protects a magnificent wilderness, containing more than 30 interconnected lakes and 900 islands, as well as vast expanses of ecologically rich, north-country forests. More than one-third of the park's surface area consists of water: parts of Rainy, Namakan, and Sand Point lakes, along the U.S.-Canada border; all of 25-mile-long, island-dotted Kabetogama Lake; and the smaller lakes and ponds. In fact, the park is named for the late 18th- and early 19th-century French-Canadian *voyageurs*, hundreds of whom traveled back and forth on these waters on their 3,000-mile trek between Montreal and Lake Athabaska and beyond. These hardy men paddled large, birchbark freight canoes loaded with great quantities of beaver pelts and other furs.

Today, the magical labyrinth of waterways offers virtually limitless opportunities to explore this park by canoe, kayak, or boat. Visitors, for example, who travel along the northern shore of the Kabetogama Peninsula, a 100,000-acre, forested and lake-dotted area between Rainy and Kabetogama lakes, will see "fleets" of wooded islands—some only an acre or less in size, and others two or three miles long. The peninsula's shore consists of an endlessly fascinating array of inlets, coves, bays, and rocky points. On the peninsula itself, chains of forest-bordered, inland lakes are reached by portage routes and other trails—the most popular of which is the Chain of Lakes Scenic Trail.

Although the sheer number of winding waterways, lakes, and islands is this park's foremost attribute, its land areas are also fascinating. The rocky hills, ridges, shore cliffs, and sloping ledges are composed of the Canadian Shield granite—part of the 1.8-million-square-mile Precambrian land mass that extends far to the north and east in Canada. Dating back more than two *billion* years, the shield's ancient sediments are among the oldest exposed rock on earth. Over the past one million years, at least four periods of continental glaciers have overlain this region of North America. The most recent period of Pleistocene Epoch glaciation, occurring within the last 30,000 years, spread ice up to two miles thick across some 4.8 million square miles of northern North America. Numerous shallow basins and other low-lying places, which were gouged out by the Laurentide Ice Sheet, are now occupied by the park's hundreds of sparkling lakes. Beaver ponds, cattail marshes, cedar swamps, and black-spruce bogs add to the diversity of habitats that support an abundance of wildlife, such as bears, moose, deer, wolves, beavers, otters, eagles, ospreys, and loons.

OUTSTANDING FEATURES

Among the many outstanding features of the park are the following: **Kabetogama, Rainy, Namakan,** and **Sand Point lakes**, the largest bodies of water in the park; **Ellsworth Rock Gardens**, a delightful picnic spot on the south shore of Kabetogama Peninsula featuring the remains of this 1940s garden of flower beds and rock sculptures; **Kettle Falls Historic District**, a waterway hub in the northeastern end of the park that was used by Indians, voyageurs, lumbermen, fishermen, and Prohibition-era bootleggers smuggling liquor from Canada and where today there are a historic dam, a dam-tender's cabin, and the Kettle Falls Hotel dating from 1912; **Little American Island**, a once-active mine site at the northwestern end of the park where the discovery of gold in the 1890s set off a short-lived gold rush; **Hoist Bay**, an area on Namakan Lake near the southern edge of the park, where traces of log hoist docks remain as a reminder of the former booming lumber industry; and **Kabetogama Peninsula**, the forested, lake-dotted wilderness heart of the park.

57

When to Go

The park is open year-round. In late spring and early summer, as bird songs fill the forests, spring rains mix with periods of gradually warming sunshine. In summer, average high temperatures remain below 80 degrees, with scattered cooler days of rain. Early autumn usually brings days of bright sunshine with a refreshing nip in the air, as the vibrant colors of autumn foliage reach their peak. As for winter, visitors should keep in mind that International Falls, just to the west of the park, is known as the "icebox of the nation." Winter, with its bitter-cold, sub-zero temperatures, strong winds, and snowstorms, is a potentially life-threatening force, although the park does offer winter activities for persons who are well-equipped. The interior of the park is inaccessible from around mid-November to late-December, when the lakes freeze over, and is again inaccessible in April, when lake ice becomes hazardous as it thaws and breaks up.

How to Get There

By Car: From U.S. Route 53 at International Falls, drive east 12 miles on State Route 11 to Rainy Lake Visitor Center. From U.S. Route 53, drive north two miles on County Route 122 and east one mile to the Kabetogama Lake Visitor Center. From U.S. Route 53, drive east eight miles on the County Route 129 (Ash River Trail) to the Ash River entrance and north three miles to the Ash River Visitor Center. From U.S. Route 53 at Orr, drive northeast about 25 miles on County Routes 23 and 24 to the Crane Lake Information Station.

By Air: Scheduled airlines serve Hibbing and International Falls, Minnesota, and Fort Frances, Ontario, Canada.

By Train: Amtrak (800-872-7245) has stops in St. Paul and Detroit Lakes, Minnesota.

By Bus: Greyhound Lines (800-231-2222) has stops in Hibbing, Minnesota.

Fees and Permits

No entrance fee is charged, and permits are not required for backcountry camping

although it is always wise to register your itinerary with the National Park Service. A state license is required for fishing in park waters. A provincial license is required if fishing in Canadian waters.

Transportation within the Park

Visitors may travel by private boats, rental boats, or float-planes or on concession-run tour cruises. Boats, canoes, outfitting, guide, and shuttle services are available at the four resort communities of Rainy Lake, Kabetogama, Ash River, and Crane Lake. In winter, the seven-mile-long Rainy Lake Ice Road provides automobile access into the park. Winter travel elsewhere is by cross-country skis, snowshoes, or snowmobile. Equipment rentals are available at local resorts.

The National Park Service provides open boats and canoes free of charge for day and overnight trips on the following interior lakes on Kabetogama Peninsula: Locator, Quill, Ek, Cruiser, Little Shoepack, Shoepack, Brown, and Peary. Their overnight use is limited to two days and one night. These watercraft are available on a first-come, first-served basis. Reservations can be made a week in advance by contacting a visitor center, where a visitor-use agreement is signed and a key is obtained. Water taxi service is available to trailheads. The 68-mile canoe loop around Kabetogama Peninsula, usually requiring five days to a week, circles around the peninsula's magnificently scenic shoreline and islands. Various segments of the loop provide outstanding canoeing opportunities.

Visitor Centers and Information Station

Rainy Lake Visitor Center: open daily year-round. Interpretive exhibits, audiovisual programs, publications, maps, navigational charts, and schedules.

Kabetogama Lake Visitor Center: open daily from early May through September. Interpretive exhibits, audiovisual programs, publications, maps, navigational charts, and schedules.

Ash River Visitor Center: open daily from early May through September. Interpretive exhibits, audiovisual programs, publications, maps, navigational charts, and schedules.

Crane Lake Information Station: open daily from late May to early September. Information, publications, maps, and navigational charts.

Facilities

Available are boat ramps and marked hiking, portaging, and cross-country skiing trails. Seasonally, available are lodging, restaurant, boat fuel, camping supplies, and mechanized portage between Rainy and Namakan lakes for boats under 21 feet.

Handicapped Accessibility

Kabetogama Lake and Rainy Lake visitor centers, half of the Oberholtzer self-guided nature trail, restrooms, and parking are wheelchair-accessible. Boat tours are accessible, with assistance. Contact the park for a detailed brochure. Braille park brochures and captioned audiovisual films are also available upon request from visitor centers.

Medical Services

First aid is available from rangers. The closest hospitals are in International Falls, 13 miles west of the Rainy Lake Visitor Center, and in Cook, 42 miles from Crane Lake.

Pets

Pets are permitted only in Rainy Lake, Kabetogama Lake, Kettle Falls, and Ash River visitor center areas, and they must be on leashes not to exceed six feet. Pets are not permitted on trails, in the backcountry, or in public buildings.

Safety and Regulations

For your safety and enjoyment and for the protection of the park, please follow these regulations and suggestions:

- The National Park Service advises that visitors travel in groups and leave a detailed itinerary with others.

- Stay abreast of current weather conditions for all activities. Understand what hypothermia is and how to avoid and deal with it.

- Remember that feeding, disturbing, capturing, hunting, or trapping wildlife, as well as damaging or cutting trees or other plantlife, taking away cultural artifacts, and carrying firearms, are prohibited.

- Please respect private property within the park and do not trespass.

- Practice minimum-impact and bear-country camping techniques.

- Visitors should comply with all state and federal boating regulations and read boating information, available at visitor centers.

The National Park Service asks that visitors not litter the park and haul out all trash from backcountry trips. Remember the excellent slogan to "leave only footprints" as a guide to help protect this national park.

Before going ashore in Canada and upon returning to the United States, visitors must report to customs offices. You and your boat can clear Canada customs at Portage Bay, on Sand Point Lake, or at International Falls bridge, on Rainy Lake. When returning, you can clear U.S. Customs at the Crane Lake Public Landing or at International Falls bridge.

ACTIVITIES

Options include canoeing, portaging, kayaking, sailing, boating, houseboating, naturalist-guided boat cruises and canoe trips, concession tour-boat trips, boat camping, swimming, water-skiing, fishing, hiking, birdwatching, interpretive nature walks and talks, children's and evening programs, camping, cross-country skiing, snowshoeing, snowmobiling, driving a lake-ice route, ice fishing, and winter camping. Further information is provided in the park's newspaper, *Rendezvous*.

Hiking Trails

Among the park's many trails are the following: **Oberholtzer Trail**, an easy half-mile, self-guided interpretive route beginning near the Rainy Lake Visitor Center and providing views of a cattail marsh and Black Bay; **Black Bay Beaver Pond Trail**, a fairly easy .6-mile route reached by water across from Sha-Sha Resort on Rainy Lake and providing a view of a beaver pond from a rocky summit;

Echo Bay Trail, a fairly easy, 2.3-mile, self-guided interpretive route (offering cross-country skiing in winter), beginning at Northern Lights Road in the community of Kabetogama and leading through a beautiful area of aspen trees, rocky, pine-covered ridges, and beaver ponds; **Blind Ash Bay Trail**, a fairly easy, 2.5-mile route beginning at the upper parking area for Ash River Visitor Center and leading westward along a pine-covered ridge to Blind Ash Bay on this wild and beautiful stretch of Kabetogama Lake's south shore; **Jorgens Lake Trail**, a fairly easy, one-mile route on Kabetogama Peninsula, beginning at the shore of Ek Bay and leading to Jorgens Lake with a spur to Quarter Line Lake; **Cruiser Lake Trail System**, a moderately strenuous, 9.5-mile hiking/portaging route across Kabetogama Peninsula from Lost Bay to Anderson Bay and passing by or near seven inland lakes; from the Lost Bay dock, it is an easy quarter-mile to exquisite Agnes Lake or a moderate five-mile hike to Cruiser Lake; **Locator Lake Trail**, a moderate, two-mile, self-guided interpretive route on Kabetogama Peninsula, beginning at a boat dock on the north shore of Kabetogama Lake and leading to the south shore of Locator Lake, on the Chain of Lakes Scenic Trail; and **Black Bay Ski Trail**, an eight-mile loop at the west end of Kabetogama Peninsula.

OVERNIGHT STAYS

Lodging and Dining

Kettle Falls Hotel, dating from 1912, is accessible only by water. It offers hotel rooms, lakeshore housekeeping units, restaurant, saloon, guide service, boat fuel, a trading post with camping supplies, limited groceries, and gifts, and rentals of boats, canoes, and kayaks. Open from mid-May through September. Contact the hotel at P.O. Box 3131, Highway 53, International Falls, MN 56649-8904; 218-283-9821 or 800-322-0886.

More than 60 resorts, providing lodging, dining, campsites, boat rentals, and other services, are also located in or near the communities of Rainy Lake, Kabetogama, Ash River, and Crane Lake.

Camping

Approximately 120 primitive boat-in campsites and 50 houseboat sites are scattered throughout the park (check bulletin boards for possible closings of some sites) and are available on a first-come, first-served basis. They have tables, sandy tent pads, fire grates, and open pit toilets, and some have bear-proof food lockers. In addition, there are about 250 traditionally used camp sites with no facilities, including two group camp sites. There is a 14-day limit of stay at all sites.

In addition, the four resort communities of Ash River, Crane Lake, Kabetogama, and Rainy Lake and the town of International Falls provide campsites with hookups for motorhomes, trailers, and car-camping.

FLORA AND FAUNA   (Partial Listings)

Mammals: black bear, moose, whitetail deer, lynx, mountain lion (rarely), bobcat, gray (timber) wolf, coyote, red and gray foxes, fisher, pine marten, mink, river otter, weasels (shorttail, longtail, and least), porcupine, raccoon, beaver, muskrat, badger, woodchuck, snowshoe hare, striped skunk, red squirrel, and eastern and least chipmunks.

Birds: common loon, red-necked grebe, white pelican, double-crested cormorant, American bittern, great blue heron, Canada and snow geese, mallard, (black, ring-necked, and wood ducks), green-winged and blue-winged teal, wigeon, pintail, shoveler, common goldeneye, common and hooded mergansers, spotted sandpiper, woodcock, herring and ring-billed gulls, terns (common, Caspian, and Forster's), bald eagle, northern harrier, hawks (sharp-shinned, broad-winged, and red-tailed), osprey, merlin, ruffed and spruce grouse, owls (barred, great gray, snowy, long-eared, great horned, boreal, and northern hawk), ruby-throated hummingbird, belted kingfisher, flicker, woodpeckers (hairy, downy, three-toed, black-backed, and pileated), yellow-bellied sapsucker, eastern kingbird, flycatchers (great-crested, olive-sided, least, and alder), eastern wood pewee, eastern phoebe, chimney swift, swallows (tree, bank, and barn), purple martin, blue and gray jays, crow, raven, black-capped

▲ *Rocky shore, Voyageurs National Park, Minnesota*

61

and boreal chickadees, white-breasted and red-breasted nuthatches, wrens (house, winter, and marsh), golden-crowned and ruby-crowned kinglets, veery, Swainson's and hermit thrushes, robin, eastern bluebird, loggerhead and northern shrikes, catbird, brown thrasher, cedar waxwing, solitary, red-eyed, and warbling vireos; Tennessee, Nashville, northern parula; black-and-white, black-throated green, black-throated blue, blackburnian, chestnut-sided, Cape May, magnolia, yellow-rumped, bay-breasted, pine, yellow, mourning, Connecticut, and Canada warblers; ovenbird, northern waterthrush, common yellowthroat, American redstart, grosbeaks (rose-breasted, pine, and evening), rufous-sided towhee, sparrows (song, chipping, white-throated, and swamp), dark-eyed junco, snow bunting, red-winged blackbird, Baltimore oriole, scarlet tanager, pine siskin, American goldfinch, red and white-winged crossbills, common and hoary redpolls, and purple finch.

Trees, Shrubs, and Flowers: pines (eastern white, red, and jack), tamarack (larch), white and black spruces, balsam fir, northern white cedar, paper birch, speckled alder, American basswood, balsam poplar, quaking and bigtooth aspens, willows, mountain and red maples, black ash, beaked hazel, serviceberry, red osier and alternate leaf dogwoods, bush and Canada honeysuckles, dwarf juniper, wild raspberry, wild strawberry, cranberry, blueberry, Labrador tea, bearberry, leatherleaf, bog rosemary, sheep laurel, pitcher plant, sundew, thimbleberry, fireweed, sarsaparilla, marsh marigold, iris, white and red trilliums, rose twisted-stalk, trailing arbutus, bunchberry, clintonia, starflower, false lily-of-the-valley, bigleaf aster, goldenrods, showy and small yellow lady's-slippers, northern and small northern bog orchids, spotted and early coralroots, rattlesnake plantain, green adder's-mouth, heart-leaved twayblade, fairy-slipper (calypso), northern slender ladies'-tresses, small purple-fringed orchid, and small round-leaved orchis.

NEARBY POINTS OF INTEREST

The area surrounding Voyageurs National Park offers other significant natural and cultural attractions that can be enjoyed as day trips or overnight excursions. Kabetogama State Forest and Superior National Forest adjoin the park to the south. To the east, there are Superior National Forest's Boundary Waters Canoe Area, Grand Portage National Monument, Isle Royale National Park, and Quetico Provincial Park in Ontario, Canada.

WIND CAVE NATIONAL PARK

▲ Black Hills, grasslands

WIND CAVE NATIONAL PARK

CUSTER   STATE   PARK

336

Sanctuary
Trail

Rankin Ridge
Trail

Centennial
Trail

87

RANKIN RIDGE

435

Beaver Creek

LIMESTONE
CANYON

Highland Creek

Highland
Creek Trail

BOLAND
RIDGE

385

Centennial
Trail

Sanctuary
Trail

5

6

Boland
Ridge Trail

BEAVES
GULCH

GURLEY
CANYON

Centennial
Trail

5

RED
VALLEY

BLACK

HILLS

NATIONAL

FOREST

Lookout
Point Trail

Elk
Mountain
Trail

PRAIRIE DOG CANYON

Highland
Creek Trail

Elk Mountain
Campground

Visitor Center

Elevator Building

NEGRO
CANYON

Beaver Creek

5

BISON FLATS

FOSSIL
RIDGE

East Bison
Flats Trail

Cold Brook
Canyon Trail

GOBBLER RIDGE

GOBBLER
CANYON

Beaver Creek

COLD
BROOK
CANYON

To Highway 7

Gobbler Pass

101

Paved Road
Unpaved Road
Hiking Trail

0 ———— 2 Kilometers
0 ———— 2 Miles

385

To Hot Springs

WIND CAVE NATIONAL PARK

**Rural Route 1, Box 190
Hot Springs, SD 57747-9430
605-745-4600**

Established in 1903, this 28,295-acre national park in the Black Hills of western South Dakota protects one of the most complex and longest cave systems in the world, with a known length of 80 miles, and is especially famous for its intricate calcite fin formations known as boxwork. Other fascinating speleothems (cave formations) include calcite nodules, called cave popcorn; branched, upright, calcium-carbonate helictites that resemble bushes; delicate, white, aragonite crystals that resemble frost; angular calcite crystals, called dogtooth spar; and wisps of beard like strands of gypsum. The wind, for which the cave was named and by which it was discovered in 1881, rushes in and out of a natural, 15-inch-diameter opening in the ground. This wind movement, occasionally reaching speeds up to 70 miles per hour, is caused by differing atmospheric pressures within the cave and above ground. Based upon air motion measurements, cave researchers estimate that perhaps as little as 5 percent of Wind Cave's rooms and passageways have been discovered.

In addition to these geological wonders, the park also contains an ecologically rich and diverse flora and fauna that thrive on the rolling prairie grassland, ponderosa pine-covered hills and ridges, and stream-cut canyons and ravines. The ranges of many western and eastern species overlap here, at the southeastern edge of the Black Hills. Bison (buffalo), elk, pronghorn, deer, prairie dogs, and wild turkeys are among the more prominent kinds of wildlife.

OUTSTANDING FEATURES

Among the many outstanding features of the park are the following: **Boxwork**, thin, honeycomb-shaped structures of calcite that extend from cave walls and ceilings in such places as the Temple Room, Elks Room, and the Pearly

Gates; **Garden of Eden**, a stunning room near the elevator that is an ideal site for visitors with physical or time limitations; **Rankin Ridge**, an area in the northwest corner of the park that offers sweeping views of surrounding pine-covered hills and contains the park's highest point, at 5,013 feet above sea level; and **Red Valley**, a prairie grassland in the park's eastern end named for outcroppings of a red shale formation and providing views of pine-dotted Boland Ridge, which separates this valley from the vast expanse of the Great Plains to the east.

PRACTICAL INFORMATION

When to Go

The park is open year-round, and cave tours are offered daily except Thanksgiving and Christmas. Summer days range from warm to hot, with average highs in the 80s and 90s and cool, comfortable evenings. Summer thunderstorms are frequent in the Black Hills. Autumn days are frequently delightful with cool air and warm, bright sunshine. While winter days can be cold and crisp, this region is relatively mild even then because of the bright, warming sunshine, as well as the tendency for frigid arctic air masses to stay east of the Black Hills, and the frequent occurrence of warm, dry, descending Chinook winds. January is usually the coldest month; March normally has the greatest snowfall. Spring produces the most variable weather patterns, with May into June normally bringing the most precipitation of the year.

How to Get There

By Car: From Custer, drive south 18 miles on U.S. Route 385, which runs through the park. From Hot Springs, drive north seven miles on U.S. Route 385. From U.S. Route 16, drive south about 12 miles through Custer State Park on State Route 87.

By Air: Rapid City Regional Airport (605-393-9924) is served by most major domestic airlines.

By Bus: Gray Line of the Black Hills (800-456-4461) offers regional tours and trips to

Mount Rushmore and Black Hills National Forest. Jack Rabbit Lines (800-444-6287) serves Wall, Rapid City, and Pierre.

Fees and Permits

There are no entrance fees, but there are fees for cave tours and camping. A free permit, available at the visitor center, is required for backcountry camping.

Visitor Center

Wind Cave Visitor Center: open daily except Thanksgiving and Christmas.

Interpretive exhibits, audiovisual programs, publications, and cave tour tickets.

Facilities

Available are a visitor center, cave elevator, cave tour routes, trails, a picnic area, and a campground.

Handicapped Accessibility

A short cave tour for people with special needs may be arranged at the visitor center, which is wheelchair-accessible.

Medical Services

Emergency first aid is available. The closest hospital is in Hot Springs, ten miles from the park.

Pets

Pets must be physically restrained at all times and are not allowed in buildings, the backcountry, or the cave.

Safety and Regulations

For your safety and enjoyment and for the

▲ *Moonrise over prairie pond, Wind Cave National Park, South Dakota*

protection of the park, please follow these regulations and suggestions:

- Because the danger of wildfire is high throughout most of the year, visitors should build fires only in the campground and only in fire grills or camp-stoves and never leave a fire unattended.

- Off-road driving and bicycling are not permitted.

- The National Park Service warns visitors to keep a safe distance from wildlife as wild animals, especially bison, can be unpredictable.

- Remember that feeding, disturbing, capturing, or hunting wildlife and damaging or removing plantlife are prohibited.

- Visitors should be alert for rattlesnakes, poison ivy, and (in spring and early summer) ticks.

The National Park Service asks that visitors not litter the park. Remember the excellent slogan to "leave only footprints" as a guide to help protect this national park.

Inside the cave: Cave temperature is a constant 53 degrees. Visitors are advised to bring a sweater or jacket and wear low-heeled, rubber-soled walking shoes. Please avoid touching the cave's delicate formations, as they are easily broken or discolored. Smoking, eating food, and drinking beverages are prohibited.

ACTIVITIES

Options include guided cave tours, candlelight and spelunking tours, evening programs, hiking, birdwatching, picnicking, and camping. Further information is provided in the park's newspaper, *Passages*.

Cave Tours

Regular guided tours of Wind Cave are offered year-round on a scheduled basis for a fee. Cave tour tickets and information are available at the visitor center, where tours begin.

Three tours follow paved, lighted paths through underground passageways decorated with boxwork and other fascinating cave formations: The *Natural Entrance and Fairgrounds Tours* follow half-mile, one-hour routes, with 300 to 450 stair-steps. The *Garden of Eden Tour* follows a quarter-mile, one-hour route with 150 stair-steps. With assistance, persons with physical limitations can tour this route.

From mid-June to mid-August, two special tours are offered, providing a more adventur-

ous cave experience and requiring special clothing and caving gear: The *Candlelight Tour* is a one-mile, two-hour excursion in which visitors experience Wind Cave, lighting their way with hand-held candle-buckets, as did early cave explorers. The route includes places where visitors must bend, stoop, and climb stairs. Reservations are required and the minimum age is eight. The *Caving Tour* is a 3,000-foot-long, three- to four-hour excursion in which visitors experience wild cave passageways and far reaches. Physical fitness is necessary to crawl through narrow openings and tight passages. Reservations are required, and the minimum age is 16.

Hiking Trails

Among the nearly 30 miles of trails are the following: **Cold Brook Canyon Trail**, a moderately easy, 1.4-mile route beginning on the west side of U.S. Route 385, two miles south of the visitor center and following Cold Brook Canyon westward to the park boundary; **Wind Cave Canyon Trail**, a fairly easy, 1.8-mile route beginning on the east side of U.S. Route 385 (a mile north of the visitor center's southern access road) and following Wind Cave Canyon eastward through rolling prairie hills to the park boundary; this is an especially excellent hike for birdwatching; **Elk Mountain Trail**, an easy, one-mile, self-guided interpretive loop beginning a half-mile north of the visitor center and leading across a stretch of prairie and through a ponderosa pine woodland; **Lookout Point Trail**, a moderately strenuous, 2.2-mile route beginning on the east side of State Route 87 (.7-mile north of its junction with U.S. Route 385), leading across rolling prairie hills to Lookout Point, and descending to Beaver Creek; to make a 4.75-mile loop hike, this trail can be combined with a segment of Centennial Trail (part of the 111-mile Centennial Trail winding through the Black Hills, commemorating South Dakota's centennial); **Rankin Ridge Trail**, a moderately strenuous, 1.25-mile route beginning from the end of a short spur road east of State Route 87 in the northwest corner of the park and climbing through ponderosa pines to the summit of the park's highest point (a lookout tower is open to visitors, in the summer), providing a grand panorama from the Black Hills to the Great Plains; and **Boland Ridge Trail**, a strenuous, 2.7-mile climb beginning a mile north of the junction of NPS Routes 5 and 6 in the eastern end of the park and affording a panorama of the park, the Black Hills, Red Valley, and the Great Plains.

OVERNIGHT STAYS

Lodging and Dining

Lodging and dining facilities are not available within the park. Accommodations and other facilities are provided in such nearby communities as Hot Springs, Custer, and Rapid City.

Camping

Elk Mountain Campground, a mile north of the visitor center, is open from April 1 to the last Sunday in October on a first-come, first-served basis. A $10 fee per night is charged from mid-May to mid-September, when water and flush toilets are available (otherwise chemical toilets are provided). No hookups or showers are available.

Backcountry Camping

Backcountry camping, for which a free backcountry permit is required, is allowed year-round in part of the park. Fires and smoking are prohibited.

FLORA AND FAUNA (Partial Listings)

Mammals: bison (reintroduced in 1913), elk (reintroduced in 1914), mule and whitetail deer, pronghorn (reintroduced in 1914), mountain lion (rarely seen), bobcat, coyote, badger, yellowbelly marmot, porcupine, raccoon, striped skunk, longtail weasel, whitetail jackrabbit, eastern cottontail, blacktail prairie dog, thirteen-lined ground squirrel, least chipmunk, and little brown myotis (bat).

Birds: red-tailed hawk, golden eagle, kestrel, prairie falcon, sharp-tailed grouse, wild turkey, killdeer, upland and spotted sandpipers, mourning dove, great horned and burrowing owls, nighthawk, white-throated swift, woodpeckers (Lewis's, red-headed, downy, and hairy), flicker, western wood pewee, cordilleran flycatcher, western and eastern kingbirds, horned lark, swallows (violet-green, cliff, and barn), jays (pinyon, blue, and gray), black-billed magpie, crow, black-capped chickadee, red-breasted and white-breasted nuthatches, wrens (rock, canyon, and house), ruby-crowned kinglet, mountain and eastern bluebirds, Townsend's solitaire, Swainson's thrush, robin, catbird, brown thrasher, cedar waxwing, vireo (solitary, warbling, and red-eyed), warblers (orange-crowned, yellow, yellow-rumped, black-and-white, and MacGillivray's), common yellowthroat, American redstart, ovenbird, yellow-breasted chat, western tanager, black-headed and evening grosbeaks, spotted towhee, sparrows (chipping, clay-colored, vesper, lark, grasshopper, and song), lark bunting, dark-eyed junco, red-winged and Brewer's blackbirds, western meadowlark, Bullock's oriole, red crossbill, pine siskin, and American goldfinch.

Amphibians and Reptiles: blotched tiger salamander, upland chorus frog, toads (plains spadefoot, Woodehouse's, and Great Plains), western painted turtle, wandering and red-sided garter snakes, eastern yellow-bellied racer, bullsnake, and prairie rattlesnake.

Trees, Shrubs, Flowers, and Grasses: ponderosa and pinyon pines, Rocky Mountain juniper, American elm, bur oak, balsam poplar, cottonwood, quaking aspen, common chokecherry, American plum, pin cherry, boxelder, green ash, northern hawthorn, wild raspberry, sagebrush, snakeweed, golden currant, skunkbush, ground plum, rabbitberry, western snowberry, soapweed yucca, plains prickly pear cactus, cattail, cow parsnip, penstemons, cinquefoils, violets (downy yellow, prairie, yellow prairie, and Canada), early wood buttercup, phlox, stonecrop, harebell, lance-leaved bluebells, common spiderwort, bluebonnet lupine, pasqueflower, crowfoot, monkeyflower, iris, lilies (sego, mountain, and wood), primroses, prairie golden pea, locoweeds, clovers, false indigo, vetch, milkvetch, scurfpea, downy paintbrush, western wallflower, Joe-pye weed, dotted gayfeather (blazingstar), black-eyed Susan, goldenrods, purple coneflower, sunflowers, asters, buffalograss, gramas (blue, hairy, and sideoats), plains bluegrass, red threeawn, western and bluebunch wheatgrasses, little bluestem, Indian ricegrass, squirreltail, needle-and-thread, porcupine grass, big bluestem, prairie sandreed, Canada wild-rye, Indian grass, prairie cordgrass, and prairie and sand dropseed.

NEARBY POINTS OF INTEREST

The area surrounding Wind Cave National Park offers other significant natural and cultural attractions that can be enjoyed as day trips or overnight excursions. Custer State Park and Black Hills National Forest adjoin the park; Jewel Cave and Devils Tower national monuments and Mount Rushmore National Memorial are to the northwest; and Badlands National Park is to the east.

OTHER NATIONAL PARK UNITS IN THE HEARTLAND REGION

▲ *Prairie landscape, Tallgrass Prairie National Preserve, Kansas*

Other National Park Units in the Heartland Region

ILLINOIS

Lincoln Home National Historic Site

413 S. 8th Street
Springfield, IL 62701-1905
217-492-4150

For 17 years before Abraham Lincoln became president in 1861, he lived with his wife, Mary Todd, and their sons at the corner of 8th and Jackson streets. Lincoln became one of the state's most successful attorneys while living here, and continued a political career that ultimately led him to the White House.

During his time in this house, Lincoln was elected to a term in the U.S. House of Representatives, and after the famous series of debates with his opponent, Stephen A. Douglas, was elected 16th president of the United States. The historic site's visitor center, at 426 S. 7th Street, provides interpretive exhibits, programs, and publications. Tours of the restored and furnished home are available through a free ticket reservation system. The site is open daily, except Thanksgiving, Christmas, and New Year's Day. The city of Springfield is located at the junction of I-55 and U.S. Route 36.

Mormon Pioneer National Historic Trail

Long Distance Trails Office
National Park Service
P.O. Box 45155
Salt Lake City, UT 84145-0155
801-539-4094

This national historic trail extends 1,297 miles from Nauvoo, Illinois, to Salt Lake City, Utah. Under the leadership of Brigham Young, 159 Mormon pioneers used the route in 1847 to seek their new Zion. The route was eventually used by more than 70,000 emigrants traveling to Utah. Today, an automobile tour route, which approximately follows the historic trail, has been marked with signs. The national historic trail is a cooperative project of the National Park Service, U.S. Bureau of Land Management, U.S. Forest Service, state and local governmental agencies, the Mormon Trails Association, and other groups. Among the highlights along or close to this route are Scotts Bluff National Monument and Chimney Rock National Historic Site in Nebraska; and Fort Laramie National Historic Site in Wyoming.

INDIANA

George Rogers Clark National Historical Park

401 S. 2nd Street
Vincennes, IN 47591-1001
812-882-1776

This 26-acre park on the east bank of the Wabash River protects the site where 170 American and French soldiers under the command of 26-year-old Lt. Col. George Rogers Clark defeated British troops at Fort Sackville during the War for Independence. The defeat opened the way for the westward expansion of the United States. The 38-hour siege of the fort in 1779 was the culmination of Clark's heroic, exhausting military offensive nearly 180 miles into enemy territory that successfully challenged British control over the region to the north and northwest of the Ohio River. As a result of that victory, the Treaty of Paris formally ending the war placed the boundary between the United States and Canada where it is today, rather than along the Ohio River. This vast wilderness became known as the Old Northwest Territory and was later divided into the states of Ohio, Indiana, Illinois, Michigan, Wisconsin, and eastern Minnesota.

The park's most conspicuous feature is the Clark Memorial, a large, circular, Greek-style structure containing 16 Doric columns. The nearby visitor center provides interpretive

▲ *Historical farm, Lincoln Boyhood National Memorial, Indiana*

exhibits, an audiovisual program, and publications. The park is open daily, except Thanksgiving, Christmas, and New Year's Day. Access to the park is by way of the Willow Street exit from U.S. Route 41 or the 6th Street exit from U.S. Route 50.

Lincoln Boyhood National Memorial

**P.O. Box 1816
Lincoln City, IN 47552-1816
812-937-4541**

This 200-acre national memorial protects the Lincoln family farm in the forested hills of southern Indiana where Abraham Lincoln lived during most of his formative years, from age seven to 21. In 1816, Abraham's father, Thomas, moved his family from Kentucky, across the Ohio River, and into the forested wilderness of the newly established state of Indiana. With the help of neighbors, the Lincolns cleared the land, built a log cabin, and planted crops. When Abraham was nine years old, his mother, Nancy, died. The following year, his father married Sarah Bush Johnston, a cheerful woman who had three children of her own, yet lovingly treated Abraham and his sister, Sarah, as her own. When Abraham was 19, the death of his sister so saddened him that he went on a three-month trip down the Ohio and Mississippi rivers to New Orleans, helping a friend navigate a flatboat loaded with livestock and farm produce. In 1830, his father sold the farm and moved to Illinois, where Abraham lived until he was elected president of the United States in 1861.

The memorial features a re-created log cabin and other structures that provide the setting for living-history programs portraying the Lincoln family's life on the farm. The visitor center provides interpretive exhibits, programs, and publications. One of the memorial's trails is a self-guided interpretive loop. Limited

73

picnicking facilities are provided, and a campground is located in a nearby state park. The memorial is open daily, except Thanksgiving, Christmas, and New Year's Day. Access to the memorial is east two miles from Gentryville on State Route 162; or south four miles from I-64 at Dale on U.S. Route 231 to State Route 162.

IOWA

Effigy Mounds National Monument

151 Highway 76
Harpers Ferry, IA 52146-7519
319-873-3491

This 1,481-acre monument, located along the bluffs above the Mississippi River in northeast Iowa, protects more than 190 pre-Columbian Indian burial mounds of a type unique in North America. While mound-builder Indians lived throughout most of the eastern United States and Canada, only in this part of Iowa, adjacent Minnesota, southern Wisconsin, and northern Illinois were mounds built in the shapes of birds and other animals. Individual burial sites are from two to four feet high and up to 137 feet long and 70 feet wide. Radiocarbon dating of artifacts, tools, and human remains in the mounds has determined that the building of the effigy mounds was practiced for more than 2,000 years—from around 550 B.C. to around A.D. 1525. During that span of time, say archaeologists, three consecutive groups of Woodland Indians—the Red Ochre, the Hopewell, and the Effigy Mounds—inhabited this area.

The monument's visitor center provides interpretive exhibits, a film, and publications. Interpreter-guided walks and other programs are offered in season. Eleven miles of trails, including self-guided interpretive routes, wind through the area and offer beautiful views of the Mississippi. Birdwatching is popular, especially in spring and early summer. The monument is located three miles north of Marquette, Iowa, on State Route 76. The area is open daily, except Thanksgiving, Christmas, and New Year's Day.

Herbert Hoover National Historic Site

Parkside Drive and Main Street
P.O. Box 607
West Branch, IA 52358-0607
319-643-2541

This 186-acre national historic site protects and interprets properties relating to the life of Herbert Hoover (1874-1964)—mining engineer, humanitarian, statesman, and the 31st president of the United States. Included at the site are the restored, two-room cottage at Downey and Penn streets where Hoover was born on August 10, 1874; a blacksmith shop owned by his father; a one-room schoolhouse, dating from 1853; a Quaker meeting house, where the Hoovers worshipped; the Hoover Presidential Library-Museum; the graves of President and Mrs. Hoover; and a 76-acre prairie.

The site's visitor center provides interpretive exhibits, audiovisual programs, and publications. Walking tours are offered, and a picnic area is available. In the summer, blacksmithing demonstrations are presented. In winter, when there are favorable conditions, cross-country skiing is popular. A picnic area is available. Access to the site from I-80's exit 254 is west 40 miles from Davenport or ten miles east from Iowa City; then north a half-mile to the visitor center at Main Street and Parkside Drive in West Branch.

KANSAS

Brown v. Board of Education National Historic Site

424 S. Kansas Avenue
Suite 220
Topeka, KS 66603-3441
785-354-4273

On May 17, 1954, the Supreme Court announced its unanimous decision in the case of *Oliver Brown, et al v. Board of Education*. "We conclude that in the field of public education the doctrine of 'separate but equal' has no place. Separate educational facilities are inherently unequal."

Brown v. Board of Education National Historic Site commemorates the Supreme Court decision at the Monroe School in Topeka, Kansas. Linda Brown, the daughter of the lead plaintiff, attended this once segregated school and, along with the other plaintiffs, was represented before the Supreme Court by Thurgood Marshall. Marshall later became the first African American to serve on the Supreme Court.

The Monroe School is currently being renovated. In the meantime, the visitor center is located on the second floor of the main post office building at 424 South Kansas Avenue, Suite 215. The park is open Monday through Friday from 8 a.m. to 5 p.m. and closed on federal holidays. Park rangers are available to answer questions and provide information about the case. There are exhibits and audiovisual programs. Tours of the school are available as conditions permit.

The site is located 55 miles west of Kansas City, Missouri, via Interstate-70. The Monroe School, 1515 Monroe Street, is about one mile south at the corner of 15th and Monroe streets, S.E.

Fort Larned National Historic Site

Route 3
Larned, KS 67550-9733
316-285-6911

This 718-acre national historic site protects and interprets a key U.S. military outpost that was established in 1859 on one of America's most important overland routes, the Santa Fe Trail. Infantry and cavalry troops from Fort Larned, including a troop of black "Buffalo Soldiers," provided protection for mail coaches and other traffic on the trail. The troops were also involved in the Indian War of 1868-69 as the Southern Plains tribes fought back in a vain attempt to preserve their land and their way of life. The fort served as an agency of the Indian Bureau from 1861-68.

Today, the nine restored original buildings surrounding the parade ground and its 100-foot tall flagstaff make up one of the best remaining examples of a frontier military post.

A visitor center located in one of the historic barracks provides interpretive exhibits, an audiovisual program, and publications. A self-guided tour leads visitors through the post's officers' quarters, a restored barracks, hospital, bakery, blacksmith shop, carpentry shop, commissary, school room, and quartermaster storehouse. The National Park Service presents living-history demonstrations. A picnic area is available, and a trail leads visitors through a stretch of restored shortgrass prairie. Wildlife species include prairie dogs, coyotes, and burrowing owls. The site is open daily, except Thanksgiving, Christmas, and New Year's Day. Access is west six miles from Larned on State Route 156.

Fort Scott National Historic Site

P.O. Box 918
Fort Scott, KS 66701-0918
316-223-0310

This 16-acre national historic site in eastern Kansas protects and interprets the reconstructed and restored buildings of this important U.S. military post established in 1842. Fort Scott was one of nine outposts initially founded to keep peace on the so-called "Permanent Indian Frontier," along the eastern edge of the Great Plains and extending from Louisiana to Minnesota. To the east of this line was the white man's territory; to the west was the declared Indian domain, extending across the vast (buffalo (bison)) grasslands of the Great Plains. The site chosen for the fort was near the eastern edge of the tallgrass prairie, on a bluff overlooking the Marmation River and Mill Creek, which are tributaries of the Osage and Missouri rivers. The fort's structures faced a large, central parade ground and included officers' quarters, barracks for the infantrymen and dragoons, a hospital, a guardhouse, and stables for the dragoons' horses. Farther back were such buildings as the quartermaster storehouse, the post's headquarters, blacksmith shop, and bakery.

From the start, Fort Scott dragoons were assigned to join the dragoons of Fort Leavenworth on the Missouri River to the north in providing armed escort for commercial caravans and emigrant wagon trains traveling southwestward on the Santa Fe Trail. In 1844, Fort Scott and Fort Leavenworth dragoons, under the command of Col. Stephen W. Kearny, joined forces in a three-month, 2,200-mile trek to demonstrate U.S. military strength and discourage British and Mexican territorial ambitions on the region. The men rode westward up the Oregon Trail, cut southward along the eastern edge of the Rocky Mountains, and looped back across the Great Plains on the Santa Fe Trail. After the policy of a permanent Indian frontier was officially terminated, Fort Scott was shut down and sold off to private interests. However, during the Civil War the post was reactivated and greatly enlarged, becoming an important supply center for Union armies in the West. In the 1870s, the U.S. Army again returned to the town of Fort Scott, this time to protect workers building a railroad across the Great Plains.

The site's visitor center, situated in the restored hospital building, provides interpretive exhibits, an audiovisual program, and publications. Other exhibits are presented in one of the restored officers' quarters and in the reconstructed dragoon barracks. Self-guided tours of the fort's 20 buildings are available, and living-history reenactments are sometimes presented. A picnic area is available. Parts of the site are being restored to natural tallgrass prairie habitat. Fort Scott is open daily, except Thanksgiving, Christmas, and New Year's Day. Access to the site is from U.S. Routes 69 or 54, which intersect in the center of town.

Nicodemus National Historic Site

c/o Fort Larned National Historic Site
Route 3
Larned, KS 67550
316-285-6911

The town of Nicodemus was settled in 1877 by a group of African Americans from Kentucky who sought a better life on the plains of Kansas. Despite many hardships and disappointments, especially the failure of the town to attract a railroad, Nicodemus survived and

today is one of the oldest, continuously occupied black towns in the West. Five historic buildings comprise the park: the African Methodist Episcopal Church, First Baptist Church, St. Francis Hotel, Nicodemus School District Number One, and Township Hall. Although the town may be toured anytime by car or on foot, the park is still under development, and facilities are limited. The National Park Service operates a part-time visitor center in the Township Hall, but the other historic buildings are closed to the public. Call for current operating schedule. Access is by way of U.S. Route 24.

Santa Fe National Historic Trail

Long Distance Trails Group Office
National Park Service
P.O. Box 728
Santa Fe, NM 87504-0728
505-988-6888

This national historic trail extends 1,200 miles from Old Franklin, Missouri; through Kansas, Oklahoma, and Colorado to Santa Fe, New Mexico. The route was initially a major 19th-century commercial and cultural link between the United States and Mexico.

There are currently 20 certified Santa Fe National Historic Trail sites and sections open to the public. The automobile highway tour route approximately following the trail is marked with the official trail logo. More than 50 federal, state, county, and municipal government agencies, private organizations, and private landowners are working cooperatively with the National Park Service on the trail project. Highlights along the trail include Pecos National Historical Park and Fort Union National Monument in New Mexico, Bent's Old Fort National Historic Site in Colorado, and Fort Larned National Historic Site in Kansas. Interpretive programs and exhibits include the Santa Fe Trail Center in Larned, Kansas; the National Frontier Trails Center in Independence, Missouri; the Santa Fe Trail Museum in Trinidad, Colorado; and the Morton County Historical Society Museum in Elkhart, Kansas.

Tallgrass Prairie National Preserve

Route 1, Box 14
Strong City, KS 66869
316- 273-8494

This 10,894-acre national preserve in the Flint Hills of east-central Kansas, protects a scenic, ecologically rich area of rolling grasslands and prairie streams (on the former Z Bar/Spring Hill Ranch). It is a nationally significant remnant of native tallgrass prairie that once covered 250 million acres of the eastern Great Plains, stretching from North Dakota to Texas. More than 150 species of birds and 20 kinds of mammals have been recorded here, along with a large variety of grasses and wildflowers. In years of adequate precipitation, the tallest of the grasses can grow to around six feet in height. The preserve also protects and interprets a number of late-19th-century buildings, including a ranch house and one-room schoolhouse, both of which are listed on the National Register of Historic Places.

Beginning at least as early as the 1930s, proposals for protecting an ecologically viable remnant of eastern Great Plains tallgrass prairie were repeatedly advocated by scientists and conservationists. In the early 1960s, a 57,000-acre Prairie National Park was proposed for an area in the Flint Hills, just north of Manhattan, Kansas. In the 1980s, an area of 50,000 acres, in northeast Oklahoma's Osage Hills, was proposed as a national preserve. All of those proposals were unsuccessful.

Finally, in 1996, after a decade of advocacy and negotiations by the National Parks and Conservation Association and the National Park Trust, the Z Bar/Spring Hill Ranch was established as the Tallgrass Prairie National Preserve. The area was also designated as a National Historic Landmark. Under a private-public partnership, the National Park Trust (a private land conservancy founded by NPCA and dedicated to purchasing and protecting nationally significant lands for inclusion in the National Park System) owns the property; while the National Park Service, under a special agreement, is cooperatively managing the preserve for resource protection and public enjoyment. Limited interpretive programs and visitor services are currently available, including a 1.75-mile self-guiding nature trail. Access to the preserve is two miles north of U.S. Route 50 at Strong City, on State Route 177.

The preserve's grasses include big and little bluestems, Indian grass, prairie dropseed, switch grass, buffalo grass, and sideoats grama. Just a few of the wildflowers are button blazingstar, various species of the pea family, verbena, compassplant, butterfly milkweed, goldenrods, prairie coneflower, and sunflowers. The few trees include eastern red cedar, American sycamore, American elm, hackberry, osage-orange, black walnut, bur oak, eastern cottonwood, eastern redbud, and honey locust. Mammals include whitetail deer, bobcat, coyote, and badger. Birds include great blue heron, killdeer, upland sandpiper, greater prairie-chicken, bobwhite, northern harrier, red-tailed hawk, kestrel, great horned owl, belted kingfisher, mourning dove, red-headed and downy woodpeckers, flicker, scissor-tailed flycatcher, eastern kingbird, eastern phoebe, eastern wood pewee, horned lark, barn swallow, blue jay, blacked-capped chickadee, house wren, eastern bluebird, robin, loggerhead shrike, catbird, mockingbird, brown thrasher, red-eyed and warbling vireos, yellow-rumped and yellow warblers, common yellowthroat, red-winged blackbird, eastern meadowlark, Baltimore oriole, lark, grasshopper and song sparrows, lapland longspur, dark-eyed junco, rose-breasted grosbeak, indigo bunting, cardinal, house finch, American goldfinch, and dickcissal.

MICHIGAN

Keweenaw National Historical Park

P.O. Box 471
Calumet, MI 49913-0471
906-337-3168

This two-unit national historical park, encompassing parts of Calumet and Laurium in Michigan's Upper Peninsula, commemorates and interprets the heritage of the oldest-known metal mining area in the western hemisphere and the earliest significant copper mine in the United States. The Keweenaw Peninsula is believed to be the only place in the world where commercially plentiful deposits of pure, native copper occurred. Mine shafts reached more than 9,000 feet underground.

In Calumet's historic business district, the park features such historic structures as the Calumet & Hecla (C&H) Mining Company general offices, dating from 1897, at 100 Red Jacket Road; the C&H Library, dating from 1897 and once containing the third largest collection of books in Michigan, across the street from the general offices; and the Red Jacket Town Hall and 1,000-seat Opera House, dating from 1886, at 340 Sixth Street. In Laurium, the park includes a number of historically and architecturally significant privately owned houses (the National Park Service and Keweenaw Tourism Council ask that visitors respect the privacy of the owners). The Thomas Hoatson house, dating from 1908, at 320 Tamarack, is the most impressive of these historic houses. This house is now known as the Laurium Manor Inn, a bed-and-breakfast facility that also offers daily tours on the hour from noon to 3 p.m. For reservations and information, call 906-337-2549.

As of this writing, the park does not yet have visitor services, but visitors are urged to obtain information at the Keweenaw Tourism Office at the intersection of U.S. Route 41 and State Route 26 in Calumet.

North Country National Scenic Trail

National Park Service
700 Rayovac Drive, Suite 100
Madison, WI 53711
608-264-5610

This national scenic trail extends 3,200 miles, from Crown Point, New York, westward through New York's Adirondack Mountains, Pennsylvania, Ohio, Michigan, Wisconsin, and Minnesota, to the Missouri River in North Dakota. The trail runs through Pictured Rocks National Lakeshore in Michigan's Upper Peninsula. Approximately half the trail is currently open to the public for hiking, cross-country skiing, and (in a few places) horseback riding.

Pictured Rocks National Lakeshore

P.O. Box 40
Munising, MI 49862-0040
906-387-3700

This protected area of 73,235 acres along the Lake Superior shore of Michigan's Upper Peninsula is the oldest national lakeshore in the United States. Among the scenic highlights are a spectacular, 15-mile stretch of 50- to 200-foot-high, sheer sandstone cliffs and the pine-framed, weather-sculpted rock formations called Miners Castle. An additional 25 miles of lakeshore includes Twelvemile Beach and the impressive Grand Sable Dunes.

Scattered inland are sparkling lakes and ponds, such as Chapel, Beaver, Little Beaver, and Grand Sable, along with marshes, bogs, streams, and a number of waterfalls. Wild forests of coniferous and deciduous trees offer a rich habitat for many species of wildlife. Mammals include whitetail deer, black bear, lynx, bobcat, gray wolf, red fox, fisher, pine marten, mink, river otter, longtail and shorttail weasels, snowshoe hare, beaver, muskrat, porcupine, raccoon, striped skunk, red and gray squirrels, and eastern chipmunk. More than 200 species of birds recorded in the area include common loon, Canada goose, great blue heron, bald eagle, osprey, ruffed and spruce grouse, great horned owl, belted kingfisher, woodpeckers (pileated, red-headed, downy, and hairy), blue jay, black-capped chickadee, white-breasted and red-breasted nuthatches, winter wren, thrushes (wood, Swainson's, and hermit), veery, red-eyed vireo, warblers (Nashville, parula, yellow-rumped, magnolia, black-throated blue, black-throated green, blackburnian, black-and-white, yellow, yellowthroat, and Canada), American redstart, ovenbird, rose-breasted grosbeak, white-throated sparrow, scarlet tanager, and purple finch. Trees include pines (white, red, and jack), tamarack (larch), white and black spruces, eastern hemlock, balsam fir, beech, northern red oak, yellow and paper birches, quaking and bigtooth aspens, and red and sugar maples. Of the great variety of shrubs and wildflowers, there are Labrador tea, bog laurel, bog rosemary, wood lily, iris, trailing arbutus, bloodroot, white trillium, starflower, pitcher plant, sundew, partridgeberry, bearberry,

79

▲ *Pictured rocks near Mosquito River, Pictured Rocks National Lakeshore, Michigan*

columbine, bottle gentian, fireweed, violets, marsh marigold, and many orchids, including lady's-slippers, coralroots, calypso, arethusa, small purple fringed, and leafy northern green.

Hiking trails, including the 43-mile Lakeshore Trail (a segment of the North Country National Scenic Trail), lead through the national lakeshore. Motorized and other wheeled vehicles, pets, and pack animals are prohibited on the backcountry trails. The National Park Service cautions visitors to keep a safe distance from cliff edges and reminds waders, swimmers, and boaters that the waters of Lake Superior are ice-cold. Campgrounds and hike-in campsites are available (a free backcountry permit is required for the latter). Lake Superior boat tours offer a great way to view the Pictured Rocks and are available in nearby Munising from June through early October. Canoeing and small-boating are enjoyable on Grand Sable Lake and the Beaver lakes. Cross-country skiing and snowshoeing are popular in winter. Public hunting is permitted in part of the national lakeshore during the designated season. Access is from Munising at the west end of the lakeshore and from Grand Marais just to the east. The partly paved County Road H58 that links the two cities also provides road access to such places as Miners Castle, Chapel Basin, the Beaver lakes, Twelvemile Beach, and Grand Sable Lake.

Sleeping Bear Dunes National Lakeshore

9922 Front Street, Highway M72
Empire, MI 49630-9797
616-326-5134

This 71,189-acre national lakeshore protects an area of massive sand dunes, high bluffs, and sandy beaches along the Lake Michigan shore in the northwest corner of Michigan's Lower Peninsula. A richly forested area, containing sparkling lakes, marshes, bogs, and streams, extends inland. North and South Manitou Islands, which are reached by ferry from Leland during the summer months, lie about seven miles offshore.

The Sleeping Bear Dunes area presents fascinating geological evidence of several periods: the Pleistocene continental glaciation of this region of North America, occurring less than 20,000 years ago; the subsequent differ-

ent levels of Lake Michigan; and the lower levels of the land as it has been slowly rebounding after being crushed beneath the tremendous weight of the glacial ice mass. This process of the land's rebounding is continuing, 11,000 years after the disappearance of the continental ice. Bays of Lake Michigan and the smaller lakes now occupy low areas and potholes, created as great concentrated chunks of the glacial ice slowly melted. Ridges of gravel and rocks, known as moraines, were formed around the edges of the glacier's outer lobes. As the bluffs and headlands along Lake Michigan have been gradually eroded, the prevailing westerly winds off the lake have carried and continue to carry the grains of sand inland, re-depositing them as the massive sand dunes that are "perched" on top of the ridges, just behind the bluffs.

The national lakeshore's varied topography and soil types support a diversity of flora and fauna. Of the mammals, there are white-tail deer, black bear, bobcat, red and gray foxes, mink, weasels, beaver, muskrat, porcupine, opossum, raccoon, striped skunk, snowshoe hare, cottontail, squirrels (red, fox, and gray), and eastern chipmunk. Birds include common loon, great blue heron, Canada goose, mallard, black and wood ducks, green-winged and blue-winged teal, wigeon, common merganser, red-tailed hawk, kestrel, ruffed grouse, Virginia and sora rails, coot, killdeer, spotted and semipalmated sandpipers, piping plover, woodcock, common snipe, herring and ring-billed gulls, mourning dove, belted kingfisher, hairy and downy woodpeckers, flicker, eastern kingbird, eastern phoebe, eastern wood pewee, swallows (tree, bank, and barn), blue jay, black-capped chickadee, white-breasted nuthatch, wrens (house, winter, and marsh), catbird, brown thrasher, robin, thrushes (wood, hermit, and Swainson's), veery, cedar waxwing, red-eyed and warbling vireos, warblers (black-and-white, Nashville, yellow, yellow-rumped, black-throated green, chestnut-sided, pine, and palm), common yellowthroat, American redstart, ovenbird, bobolink, eastern meadowlark, red-winged blackbird, northern oriole, scarlet tanager, rose-breasted and evening grosbeaks, indigo bunting, American goldfinch, rufous-sided towhee, and savannah, vesper, tree, chipping, white-throated, swamp, and song sparrows.

Among the trees are pines (white, red, and jack), tamarack (larch), black spruce, eastern hemlock, balsam fir, northern white cedar, common juniper, beech, white and northern red oaks, yellow and paper birches, American basswood, cottonwood, quaking and bigtooth aspens, red and sugar maples, and green, white, and black ashes. Shrubs and wildflowers include staghorn sumac, creeping juniper, bearberry, false heather, partridgeberry, searocket, beach pea, rock sandwort, puccoon, wood lily, harebell, evening primrose, bunchberry, low blueberry, lance-leaved coreopsis, spotted and striped coralroots, fringed polygala, white trillium, pipsissewa, wintergreen, Canada mayflower, bloodroot, spring beauty, hepatica, yellow trout lily, yellow violet, false Solomon's seal, columbine, cardinal flower, jack-in-the-pulpit, orange hawkweed, black-eyed susan, goldenrods, swamp loosestrife, pink pyrola, marsh marigold, arrowhead, and waterlily.

The Philip A. Hart Visitor Center, on State Route 72 just east of the village of Empire, provides interpretive exhibits, an audiovisual program, and publications. The Sleeping Bear Point Coast Guard Station Maritime Museum presents exhibits on Great Lakes maritime history, and a small visitor center is located on South Manitou Island. The National Park Service provides a variety of interpretive programs and ranger-led walks. A number of drives lead to points of interest, including the 7.5-mile, self-guided interpretive Pierce Stocking Scenic Drive that affords excellent views of the dunes and Lake Michigan. More than a dozen hiking trails, ranging from easy to strenuous, offer interesting and scenic excursions onto the dunes, bluffs, and moraines, and through richly forested areas. In winter, a few of these routes are excellent for cross-country skiing.

Canoeing is a favored activity, and canoe rentals are available. Swimming is popular in summer, but visitors are cautioned to be careful of the surf along the Lake Michigan beaches. Picnic areas are available at several places. Camping facilities are provided at Platte River Campground, for which reservations for the June 25 to September 6 season can be made by contacting the National Park Reservation Service at 800-365-CAMP. Backcountry camping is on a first-come, first-served basis at designated sites on the mainland and on both Manitou islands; a permit is required and fees are charged. Public hunting is permitted in part of the lakeshore during the designated season. Access to the national lakeshore is west 25 miles from Traverse City by way of U.S. Route 31, State Route 72, or State Route 22; or from Muskegon by way of U.S. Route 31.

MINNESOTA

Grand Portage National Monument

P.O. Box 668
Grand Marais, MN 55604-0668
218-387-2788

This 710-acre national monument on the shore of Lake Superior at the northeast tip of Minnesota protects and interprets the site of the field headquarters of the Great Lakes region's largest and most successful late 18th-century fur-trading company. The monument also includes the 8.5-mile Grand Portage, a trail that voyageurs and canoemen once used to avoid the impassable waterfalls and rapids on the Pigeon River. The North West Company's Grand Portage fur-trading headquarters, operating from 1784 to 1803, consisted of 16 buildings within a stockade; included were a Great Hall, business office, kitchen house, general store, fur store, carpentry and blacksmith shops, and dwellings for the manager and key partners. The company employed more than 1,000 canoemen, 50 traders, and several dozen guides. In late June or early July, an annual rendezvous brought together local Indians, voyageurs, and canoemen. After this gathering that included festivities and ceremonies, the men were sent forth into the north country wilderness to bring back huge quantities of beaver pelts and other furs. Their great birchbark canoes, some measuring up to 36 feet long, carried up to 8,000 pounds of pelts, furs, and other cargo on the Great Lakes and larger rivers and were paddled by eight to ten men. More maneuverable canoes, measuring around 26 feet, were used on the region's smaller rivers.

Today, the monument features the replicas of several of the post's structures, including the Great Hall and kitchen house within the stockade and the canoe-storage building, housing two birchbark canoes, outside the palisade. The Grand Portage is now a popular hiking trail in late spring, summer, and autumn and is increasingly used for cross-country skiing and snowshoeing in winter.

Hikers may be fortunate to see such wildlife as moose, whitetail deer, lynx, bobcat, red and gray foxes, wolverine, fisher, pine marten, mink, river otter, and beaver. Birds of the Grand Portage area include common loon, Canada goose, woodcock, common snipe, bald eagle, osprey, ruffed grouse, great horned owl, pileated and three-toed woodpeckers, hermit thrush, veery, numerous warblers, rose-breasted grosbeak, and purple finch. Among the trees are tamarack (larch), white and black spruces, balsam fir, northern white cedar, yellow and paper birches, quaking and bigtooth aspens, mountain ash, red and mountain maples, and white, red, and jack pines.

The monument provides interpretive exhibits and an audiovisual program in the Great Hall, as well as living-history demonstrations and an annual reenactment of the historical fur traders' rendezvous. The stockade area is open from mid-May to mid-October. A picnic area is available. Near the stockade, a half-mile trail climbs 300 feet to the summit of Mount Rose, offering views directly down to the stockade and across Grand Portage Bay to Grand Portage Island and the open expanse of Lake Superior. Summer ferry service links the monument with Isle Royale National Park. Highway access to the monument is northeast 36 miles from Grand Marais, Minnesota, on State Route 61; or southwest 43 miles from Thunder Bay, Ontario, Canada, on Ontario Route 61 and Minnesota Route 61.

Mississippi National River and Recreation Area

175 East 5th Street
Suite 418, Box 41
St. Paul, MN 55101-2901
612-290-4160

This 53,775-acre, 72-mile river corridor between Dayton and Hastings, Minnesota, was designated to increase public recognition and appreciation of this stretch of the Mississippi River as it flows through a variety of landscapes and passes important cultural, historical, and industrial features that trace the history of human activity in this region. While the National Park Service owns only about 50 acres, thousands of acres within the national river and recreation area are protected by dozens of state and local parks that provide outstanding recreational opportunities. Access is provided by a number of highways, including I-35 and I-94.

Pipestone National Monument

P.O. Box 727
Pipestone, MN 56164-0727
507-825-5464

This 281-acre national monument in southwest Minnesota protects and interprets important quarries that provided the Dakota Sioux and other Plains Indian tribes with this relatively soft, yet durable reddish stone from which they carved ceremonial pipes. This red stone, now known as *Catlinite* in honor of painter George Catlin, was valued for its durability and flexibility and is believed to have been the preferred source for pipestone since the 17th century. Pipes crafted from it were an integral part of such important tribal events as trade and peace negotiations, ceremonial dances, medicine and healing ceremonies, and preparations for warfare. While the shaping of pipe bowls began as simple, unadorned tubes, they became increasingly elaborate over time. Some were shaped into animal and human figures, and T-shaped "calumets" were traditionally used in treaty ceremonies. The long stems of the pipes were carved from hardwood, such as ash, and decorated with paint, carvings, beads, and feathers.

The quarry, which is open to limited quarrying by Indian carvers only, is reached on a three-quarter-mile loop trail. Visitors are urged to stay out of the quarry pits and to remember that it is unlawful to remove pipestone except by special permit. Visitors may observe Native American craftsmen fashioning traditional pipes from the red rock and see other craft demonstrations and displays in the Upper Midwest Indian Cultural Center.

In addition to the quarries, the monument protects a varied natural environment that includes a small remnant of gently rolling Great Plains tallgrass prairie, a small oak and ash woodland, and marsh habitat that borders Pipestone Creek and Lake Hiawatha. More than 100 species of birds recorded in the monument include mourning dove, eastern kingbird, horned lark, blue jay, house and sedge wrens, brown thrasher, catbird, yellow warbler, yellowthroat, red-winged blackbird, bobolink, meadowlark, American goldfinch, dickcissel, and tree, grasshopper, clay-colored, and song sparrows. Of the more than 300 varieties of plantlife, there are oaks, green ash, chokecherry, dotted gayfeather, purple prairie clover, goldenrod, and such grasses as prairie cordgrass, big bluestem, buffalograss, and blue and sideoats gramas. The monument and cultural center are located one mile north of the town of Pipestone.

MISSOURI

George Washington Carver National Monument

**5646 Carver Road
Diamond, MO 64840
417-325-4151**

This 210-acre national monument near Joplin, Missouri, honors the accomplishments of George Washington Carver (1864-1943), an African American who was born a slave and rose to national prominence in several fields of endeavor. Becoming exceptionally proficient in mathematics, music, and painting, he was widely acclaimed as an agronomist, botanist, humanitarian, and educator. Carver began his career as a research botanist at Iowa Agricultural College (now Iowa State University). He then joined Booker T. Washington at his Tuskegee Institute in Alabama (now commemorated as the Booker T. Washington National Monument and Tuskegee Institute National Historic Site), where Carver taught courses in agriculture and botany. Dr. Carver first gained national attention when his work in agricultural chemistry led to the extraction of many products from peanut, sweet potato, and soybean plants. His research, teaching, and writing were always motivated by his intense desire "to be of the greatest good to the greatest number of 'my people.'"

The monument's visitor center provides interpretive exhibits, audiovisual programs, and publications. On many weekends, special programs, films, and tours are offered. The three-quarter-mile Carver Trail leads visitors on a self-guided walk to the monument's high-lights, including the site of Carver's birthplace, Carver Spring, the 1881 Moses Carver House, the Carver family cemetery, and an area of tallgrass prairie that is being restored to a nat-ural condition. The monument is open daily, except Thanksgiving, Christmas, and New Year's Day. A picnic area is available. Access to the monument from I-44 is at Exit 18; drive south seven miles on U.S. Route A-71 to the town of Diamond, then west two miles on County Road V and south about a mile on Carver Road (County Road 16Q).

Harry S Truman National Historic Site

**223 N. Main Street
Independence, MO 64050-2804
816-254-9929**

This six-acre, two-unit national historic site pro-tects and interprets both the 14-room, Victorian-style house that for 53 years was the home of Harry S Truman, the 33rd President of the United States, and the Harry S Truman Farm Home in Grandview, Missouri. The house in Independence was built by Bess Truman's grandfather, and during the Truman presidency (1945-1953), it was considered the "Summer White House."

National Park Service tour tickets, issued on a first-come, first-served basis, are avail-able at the Truman Home Ticket and Information Center at Truman Road and Main Street. The center presents an audiovisual introduction to the site and is open daily, except Thanksgiving, Christmas, and New Year's Day. Other nearby Truman-related places include the Harry S Truman Library, containing exhibits and many of Truman's presidential papers. Access to the Truman Home is north from I-70 on Noland Road and west on Truman Road to the ticket center.

Access to the Truman Farm Home is south from I-435 on Route 71 and west about a mile on Blue Ridge Blvd.

Jefferson National Expansion Memorial

11 N. 4th Street
St. Louis, MO 63102-1882
314-655-1700

This 91-acre memorial on the west bank of the Mississippi River commemorates President Thomas Jefferson's soaring vision of the 19th-century westward expansion of the United States. Among Jefferson's accomplishments toward that end were his purchase of the Louisiana Territory in 1803, which doubled the size of the United States, and his sending forth in 1804 the 8,000-mile Lewis and Clark Expedition from St. Louis to Fort Clatsop, near the mouth of the Columbia River in the Oregon Territory.

Architect Eero Saarinen designed the bold, award-winning, 630-foot-tall, stainless-steel arch called the "Gateway to the West." The arch in its graceful "catenary" curve—the shape that is attained when a weighted chain is freely
suspended between two points—is a dynamic symbol and a grand memorial to the daring, determination, sacrifice, and vision of the early American explorers and pioneer settlers. The epic story of the courageous people who ventured across this vast and rugged land when so little was known about it is eloquently portrayed by interpretive exhibits and films in the Museum of Westward Expansion, located underground beneath the archway. A tram takes visitors to the top of the arch for spectacular panoramas.

In a nearby part of the national expansion memorial is the domed Old Courthouse, made famous by the trials of Dred Scott in 1847 and 1850 that led to the 1857 U.S. Supreme Court decision that, since slaves were not "persons" or citizens, they had no standing to sue and that slavery could not be restricted in the territories (not yet having attained the status of statehood). These rulings increased national tensions over slavery and helped push the nation toward Civil War. Both the memorial and the Old Courthouse are open daily, except Thanksgiving, Christmas, and New Year's Day.

Lewis and Clark National Historic Trail

National Park Service
700 Rayovac Drive, Suite 100
Madison, WI 53711
608-264-5610

This 3,700-mile trail extends from the Mississippi River in Illinois to the mouth of the Columbia River in Oregon and celebrates the

epic Lewis and Clark Expedition of 1804-1806. Roads, trails, and rivers connect the route's historic sites, which are variously managed by federal, state, and local governmental agencies as well as private organizations. National Park Service units along the route are Jefferson National Expansion Memorial in St. Louis, Missouri, Knife River Indian Villages National Historic Site in North Dakota, Nez

▲ *Gateway Arch, Jefferson National Expansion Memorial, Missouri*

Perce National Historical Park in Montana, Idaho, Oregon, and Washington, Fort Vancouver National Historic Site in Washington State, and Fort Clatsop National Memorial in Oregon.

Ozark National Scenic Riverways

P.O. Box 490
Van Buren, MO 63965-0490
573-323-4236

This oldest national scenic river in southeast Missouri protects 80,790 acres along 140 miles of the Current and Jacks Fork rivers. The rivers flow through lush forests and pass by scenic bluffs, caves, and large freshwater springs. Float trips, canoeing, boating, tubing, swimming, fishing, and cave tours are popular. Canoe and boat rentals are available, as are picnic areas and campgrounds. Many miles of former logging roads and a nine-mile stretch of the Ozark Trail provide excellent hiking opportunities. Public hunting is permitted in part of the riverways during the designated season. A number of highways lead to the area, including U.S. Route 63; State Route 72, south of Rolla; and U.S. Route 60, northwest of Poplar Bluff.

Ulysses S. Grant National Historic Site

7400 Grant Road
St. Louis, MO 63123-1801
314-842-1867

This 9.6-acre national historic site protects and interprets White Haven estate, the pre-Civil War home of the Union general and 18th U.S. president, Ulysses S. Grant. After having played a significant role in the ultimate Union victory in the Civil War, Grant was elected to the presidency in 1868 and served two terms. A visitor center provides interpretive exhibits. Ranger-led tours are offered, and a self-guided tour of the estate grounds is available. The site is open daily, except Thanksgiving, Christmas, and New Year's Day. Access from I-270 South is at the Gravois Road exit, east on Gravois Road, and north on Grant Road to the site.

Wilson's Creek National Battlefield

Route 2, Box 75
Republic, MO 65738-9514
417-732-2662

This 1,750-acre national battlefield, ten miles southwest of Springfield in southwest Missouri, protects and interprets the site of the first major Civil War battle west of the Mississippi. On August 10, 1861, 6,000 Union troops unleashed a courageous assault in the half-light of dawn, caught by surprise the 12,000 sleeping Confederate soldiers, and occupied a ridge that came to be called Bloody Hill. In the summer's oppressive heat and humidity, fierce and close combat dragged on for hours, as first one side and then the other gained control of the high ground. Amid a blizzard of bullets, casualties fell all over the hill. For a while, it appeared that the far smaller Union force would be victorious. However, with ammunition running low, the soldiers exhausted, and their commander dead, the Union force finally gave up the hill and retreated. Casualties for the day, which were about evenly divided, totaled more than 2,500 men killed, wounded, or missing. The Confederate victory here led to greater federal attention to the crises in Missouri and resulted in keeping Missouri— one of three border states that could have seceded and joined the Confederacy—in the Union.

A visitor center provides interpretive exhibits, an audiovisual program, and publications. A 4.9-mile, self-guided drive winds through the national battlefield, with interpretive stops at such places as Bloody Hill, Gibson's Mill, and the Ray House, which served as a Confederate field hospital during and after the battle. Ranger-led tours of Bloody Hill and Ray House are offered seasonally; living-history demonstrations are presented in spring, summer, and autumn. Trails lead visitors to points of interest. The national battlefield is open daily, except Thanksgiving, Christmas, and New Year's Day. Access to the battlefield from I-44 is at exit 70, south six miles on State Route MM, right onto State Route ZZ, and left onto Farm Road 182 to the battlefield entrance.

NEBRASKA

Agate Fossil Beds National Monument

301 River Road
Harrison, NE 69346
308-668-2211

Located on a former working cattle ranch, this 3,055-acre national monument along the Niobrara River in northwest Nebraska protects an amazing concentration of extremely well-preserved fossilized remains of mammals dating from around 20 million years ago. This rich paleontological site of the Miocene Epoch contains an abundance of small forms of gazelle-like camels, horses, and rhinoceroses, along with small, sheep-like oreodons, a large, boar-like creature, and the forerunners of today's cats and dogs. During this important period in the evolution of mammals, the region consisted of a lush savanna grassland environment, scattered with clumps of trees and teeming with wildlife. As the Rocky Mountains were gradually uplifted, the climate to the east became increasingly arid and vulnerable to periods of prolonged droughts, with periodic river floods from the mountains. Hundreds of the animals perished in the droughts and floods. Their remains were buried by wind-blown and water-borne sediments, in which many of their remains became fossilized.

A visitor center at the monument provides interpretive exhibits, an audiovisual program, and publications. A two-mile round-trip, self-guided interpretive trail leads from the visitor center to the University and Carnegie hills, where important early paleontological research was performed. Several trails lead through the high plains prairie and buttes carved by the meandering Niobrara River. Access to the monument from U.S. Route 25 at Mitchell, Nebraska, is north 34 miles on State Route 29; or from U.S. Route 20 at Harrison, Nebraska, south 22 miles on State Route 29.

California National Historic Trail

Long Distance Trails Office
National Park Service
P.O. Box 45155
Salt Lake City, UT 84145-0155
801-539-4094

This more than 5,600-mile trail includes mid-19th-century overland routes that in the 1840s and 1850s were used by people seeking their fortunes in gold or a new life in California. The routes begin at several locations along the Missouri River, including St. Joseph and Independence, Missouri, and Council Bluffs, Iowa, and end at a variety of sites in California and Oregon. The national historic trail is currently in the planning stage by the National Park Service and cooperating organizations. Three of the many historic highlights along the route are Scotts Bluff National Monument in Nebraska, Fort Laramie National Historic Site in Wyoming, and City of Rocks National Reserve in Idaho.

Homestead National Monument of America

Route 3, Box 47
Beatrice, NE 68310-9416
402-223-3514

By protecting and interpreting the land claim of homesteaders Daniel and Agnes Freeman, this 195-acre national monument in the farmland of southeast Nebraska honors all those who courageously moved west and became pioneer settlers in the Great Plains and the western frontier. The Freemans were among the first applicants under the Homestead Act of 1862, which provided that U.S. citizens and immigrants intending to become citizens could file a claim on 160 acres of government land if the claimants would build a home and plant crops there. If, after five years, the original claimant still occupied the land as stipulated, that person owned it free and clear. Between 1863 and 1935, more than 270 million acres of public domain lands—10 percent of the land in the United States—were deeded to homesteaders.

While the original Freeman family buildings no longer exist, the monument does feature an 1867 log-and-chink cabin that was moved from a nearby homestead and is typical of the frontier homes in eastern Nebraska. The one-room Freeman schoolhouse, dating from 1872, is located on a separate unit of the monument. A visitor center provides interpretive exhibits of historic photographs and artifacts, an audiovisual program, and publications. Ranger-led walks and living-history demonstrations are offered during the summer. A 2.5-mile, self-guided interpretive trail leads visitors to the site of the Freeman cabin and to a brick house built by the Freemans in 1876. Another trail follows Cub Creek through a wooded area and loops through a 100-acre expanse of restored tallgrass prairie (visitors are cautioned to be alert for poison ivy and ticks). Access to the monument from Beatrice is west 4.5 miles on State Route 4.

Missouri National Recreational River

P.O. Box 591
O'Neill, NE 68763-0591
402-336-3970

This two-unit national recreational river covers nearly 100 miles of the Missouri River, mostly where it forms the border between northeast Nebraska and southeast South Dakota. The upper 39-mile segment, below Fort Randall Dam near Pickstown, South Dakota, contains outstanding natural riparian woodlands and tallgrass and mixed-grass prairie. The lower 59-mile stretch, extending from Gavins Point Dam near Yankton, South Dakota, to Ponca, Nebraska, illustrates the river's constantly changing, dynamic character with its islands, sand bars, chutes, and channels. While most of the land along the river is privately owned, U.S. Army Corps of Engineers and state and local facilities provide public access. The National Park Service has no visitor facilities there at this time.

Niobrara National Scenic Riverway

P.O. Box 591
O'Neill, NE 68763-0591
402-336-3970

This 76-mile national scenic riverway focuses attention on two stretches of this beautiful and biologically important prairie river in northern Nebraska. The Niobrara (an Indian name meaning "running water") flows through an ecological crossroads between eastern woodlands and western grasslands where diverse flora and fauna represent a half-dozen major ecosystems. The upper stretch of the riverway provides outstanding opportunities for canoeing; it has, in fact, been rated as one of the top ten best canoeing rivers in the United States. Most of the land along the river is pri-

vately owned, and the National Park Service offers no facilities there at this time. Canoeing information may be obtained from the Valentine Chamber of Commerce, P.O. Box 201, Valentine, NE 69201; 800-658-4024.

Oregon National Historic Trail

Long Distance Trails Office
National Park Service
P.O. Box 45155
Salt Lake City, UT 84145-0155
801-539-4094

Extending 2,170 miles from Independence, Missouri, to Oregon City, Oregon, this historic route was used by fur traders, trappers, frontiersmen, gold-seekers, missionaries, and more than 300,000 emigrants from the 1840s through the 1850s. The trail is cooperatively managed by the National Park Service, U.S. Bureau of Land Management (BLM), U.S. Forest Service, state and local governmental agencies, and private organizations. Among the highlights are Scotts Bluff National Monument and Chimney Rock National Historic Site in Nebraska, Hagerman Fossil Beds National Monument in Idaho, and Whitman Mission and Fort Vancouver national historic sites in Washington State. Several Bureau of Land Management sites are also along the route, including Oregon National Historic Trail Corridor Sites in Wyoming, Bonneville Point Section of the Oregon Trail, which is seven miles east of Boise, Idaho, and National Historic Oregon Trail Interpretive Center, near Baker City, Oregon.

Pony Express National Historic Trail

Long Distance Trails Office
National Park Service
P.O. Box 45155
Salt Lake City, UT 84145-0155
801-539-4094

The Pony Express' mail-delivery service is celebrated by this 1,800-mile national historic trail that extends from St. Joseph, Missouri, to Sacramento, California. The service provided ten-day runs from April 1860 to October 1861. This trail is currently in the planning

89

▲ *Agate Fossil Beds National Monument, Nebraska*

stage by the National Park Service, in cooperation with other governmental agencies and private organizations. Among the many historic highlights along this route are Scotts Bluff National Monument and Chimney Rock National Historic Site in Nebraska and Fort Laramie National Historic Site in Wyoming.

Scotts Bluff National Monument

P.O. Box 27
Gering, NE 69341-0027
308-436-4340

This 3,003-acre national monument protects a weather-sculpted, sandstone formation that was an imposing witness to many phases of 19th-century westward expansion. Rising 800 feet above the North Platte River in northwest Nebraska, this great bluff was a major landmark for early fur traders, including Hiram Scott, who died near the base of the bluff in 1828 and for whom it was subsequently named. After the boom in fur trading declined, some former trappers became guides for Christian missionaries up the North Platte and on to the Oregon Territory. By the mid-1840s, a growing flow of caravans, filled with many thousands of pioneer families, traveled by Scotts Bluff on this route that came to be known as the Oregon Trail. In the late 1840s, gold was discovered in California, and suddenly a new influx of westbound travelers was passing the bluff in the form of 20,000 to 30,000 gold seekers. By 1852, tens of thousands of emigrants in their prairie schooners passed by—50,000 in just a single year. In the early 1860s, mail services, including the Pony Express, were dashing by on their way to the Pacific Coast. And in 1869, the Union Pacific Railroad constructed its line just south of Scotts Bluff, connecting with the Central Pacific Railroad in northern Utah and thereby completing the first transcontinental rail line across America.

Visitors may hike or drive the 1.6 miles to the summit of the bluff, which is 4,649 feet above sea level. The monument's visitor center, featuring the Oregon Trail Museum, provides an audiovisual program on the Oregon Trail, publications, and interpretive exhibits on historic trails and geological and archaeological aspects of the area. Also on display are his-

toric photographs and paintings by William Henry Jackson, the first person to photograph Yellowstone. A picnic area is available. The monument is located on State Highway 92, three miles west of Gering or five miles southwest of the city of Scottsbluff.

NORTH DAKOTA

Fort Union Trading Post National Historic Site

Rural Route 3, Box 71
Williston, ND 58801-9455
701-572-9083

This 443-acre national historic site in northwest North Dakota and adjacent Montana protects and interprets the site of the most important 19th-century fur-trading center in the Missouri River region. Established in 1828 by the Upper Missouri Outfit, an affiliate of the American Fur Company, the post was situated on an expanse of shortgrass prairie with a view of the river and scenic bluffs and buttes beyond. The post's palisades-enclosed quadrangle included the Bourgeois (manager's) House, a building housing company employees, an Indian trading house, a company store, storerooms, kitchen, carpentry and blacksmith shops, a gunpowder magazine, an enclosure for horses, and two stone watchtowers at opposite corners of the palisades.

The fortunes of this historic trading post rose and fell with events. Just as the post was starting its operation, beaver hats suddenly went out of fashion, so the post's founder, Kenneth McKenzie, quickly switched to buffalo robes, which he obtained from the Blackfeet, Assiniboines, and other Plains Indian tribes. Business flourished for nearly a decade, but then disaster struck. In 1837, an epidemic of the deadly, European-borne smallpox virus ravaged some of the region's Indian populations, which had little or no natural immunity to the disease. The post's trading business dramatically declined for awhile though, gradually, trading resumed and once again flourished. Then in 1857, another smallpox epidemic swept through some of the tribes, and again the Fort Union Trading Post's business plummeted—this time never to recover. In 1867, the decaying post was sold to the U.S. Army, which dismantled the buildings for reuse in expanding the military's nearby Fort Buford. The National Park Service has reconstructed some of the trading post, including the Bourgeois House, trading house, kitchen, and bastions. The visitor center, located in the Bourgeois House, provides exhibits of artifacts, other interpretive material, and publications. During the summer, ranger-led tours and living-history demonstrations are presented. From Thursday through Sunday of the third weekend in June, an annual reenactment of the fur-trading rendezvous is performed. A picnic area is available. The site is open daily, except Thanksgiving, Christmas, and New Year's Day. The site may be reached via three different routes: southwest 24 miles from Williston, North Dakota, on U.S. Route 2 and ND Route 1804; northeast 21 miles from Sidney, Montana, on MT Route 200 and ND Route 58; or about 80 miles north of Theodore Roosevelt National Park's North Unit on U.S. Route 85 and ND Routes 200 and 58.

Knife River Indian Villages National Historic Site

P.O. Box 9
Stanton, ND 58571-0009
701-745-3309

This 1,758-acre national historic site near the junction of the Knife and Missouri rivers in west-central North Dakota protects and interprets the remains of historic Hidatsa and Mandan Indian villages. By the early 18th century, these tribes of Northern Plains Indians were the thriving culmination of at least 700 years of established settlements along the upper Missouri River. Five of their summer villages, consisting of earthlodge dwellings, were perched atop terraces above the Knife and Missouri rivers. These farming villagers traded their agricultural produce with friendly nomadic tribes, while their warriors fought to protect the villages from attacks by unfriendly tribes. These settlements were also the center of widespread intertribal trading of such materials as turquoise from the Southwest, shells from the Pacific and Gulf coasts, obsidian (volcanic

glass) from the Yellowstone region, and copper from the upper Great Lakes region.

The earliest documented white person to visit these villages was a Frenchman, Pierre de la Verendrye, in 1738. The Lewis and Clark Expedition spent the winter of 1804-05 at nearby Fort Mandan, and in the 1830s painters George Catlin and Karl Bodmer produced beautiful paintings of the Indians' earthlodges and activities. But, tragically, the white explorers also inadvertently brought the smallpox virus, against which the Native Americans had little or no immunity. In 1781, this deadly scourge swept through the tribes and decimated their populations. Soon after another epidemic ravaged even more of them, the few remaining Mandan and Hidatsa people finally abandoned their villages in 1845 and established a new community upstream where, in 1862, they were joined by the Arikara Indians. In 1885, these three tribes were forced by the white settlers to leave their village and move onto the Fort Berthold Indian Reservation. Their descendants, now referred to as members of the Three Affiliated Tribes, continue to practice many of their ancient traditions.

The site's visitor center features an orientation program, interpretive exhibits, Native American crafts, publications, and a full-scale replica of an earthlodge. Ranger-led interpretive walks are offered during the summer. Self-guided interpretive walks are available, including the 1.5-mile Awatixa Trail that leads from the visitor center to Awatixa Village. Other trails, ranging from a half-mile to seven miles, lead hikers (and, in winter, cross-country skiers) through riparian woodland and prairie grassland (visitors are cautioned to be careful along unstable riverbanks). Special cultural events and demonstrations, including Native American dances, gardening, and the tanning of hides, are presented during the summer. The Northern Plains Indian Culture Fest is held during the fourth weekend in July. A picnic area is available near the visitor center. The site is open daily, except Thanksgiving, Christmas, and New Year's Day. Access to the site from I-94 at Bismarck is north 41 miles on U.S. Route 83, west 23 miles on State Route 200A, and north several miles through Stanton. From U.S. Route 2 at Minot, drive south about 50 miles on U.S. Route 83, west and south on State Route 200, and then County Route 37.

Cuyahoga Valley National Recreation Area

**15610 Vaughn Road
Brecksville, OH 44141-3018
216-650-4636**

Located between Cleveland and Akron, Ohio, in the largely wooded Cuyahoga River valley carved by continental glaciation thousands of years ago, this 32,524-acre national recreation area protects a variety of sites with natural and historical significance.

The historic Ohio & Erie Canal, for instance, completed in 1832, once provided a major transportation route between Cleveland, on the shore of Lake Erie, and Portsmouth, on the Ohio River. Stretches of the canal still contain water, and a few of the locks and other canal structures remain. The Ohio & Erie Canal Towpath Trail runs the length of the national recreation area, providing views of woodlands, marshes, and fields and opportunities for hiking, bicycling, horseback riding, and cross-country skiing. Also running the length of the area is the Cuyahoga Valley Scenic Railroad, a diesel-locomotive-powered passenger train (a fee is charged), following the historic route of the Valley Railroad that began service in the 1870s. National Park Service interpreters aboard the train present information on the natural and cultural history of the valley.

Other highlights of the area include numerous tributary streams with beautiful waterfalls, such as Brandywine Falls; the Hale Farm & Village, containing historic buildings from around the region, re-creating the lifestyle of 19th-century Ohio residents, and demonstrating crafts by glassblowers, potters, weavers, spinners, candlemakers, and blacksmiths; the Blossom Music Center, the summer home of the Cleveland Symphony Orchestra and a place where summer musical programs are presented; and the Porthouse Theater, where Shakespeare plays, Broadway musicals, drama, and opera are performed.

Three visitor centers provide interpretive exhibits, audiovisual programs, and publications: Canal Visitor Center, at Canal and Hillside roads in Valley View, is open daily, except Thanksgiving, Christmas, and New Year's Day; Happy Days Visitor Center on State Route 303 is open daily; and Hunt Farm Visitor Information Center, on Bolanz Road between Riverview and Akron-Peninsula roads, is open daily. In addition, the Frazee House presents museum exhibits on the early settlement of Cuyahoga Valley; and the Boston Store presents interpretive exhibits on the early canal-boat-building industry.

Numerous picnic sites are available in the recreation area, and visitors may also enjoy birdwatching, golf, snowshoeing, sledding, and ice-skating. Two lodging facilities are located within the area: the historic inn at Brandywine Falls that is now a bed-and-breakfast, and the Stanford Youth Hostel in the historic Stanford farmhouse. Access to the recreation area from I-80 (the Ohio Turnpike) is at Exit 11, northbound on I-77 to Rockside Road exit, east on Rockside just over one mile, and right onto Canal Road to enter the north end of the recreation area.

Dayton Aviation Heritage National Historical Park

**P.O. Box 9280, Wright Brothers Station
Dayton, OH 45409-9280
937-225-7705**

This 85-acre national historical park commemorates the pioneering research, inventions, and contributions to aviation of Orville and Wilbur Wright, as well as the life and poetry of their African-American friend and business associate, Paul Laurence Dunbar. National historic landmarks located within the park include the Wright Cycle Company Shop, at 22 S. Williams St., which the brothers opened in 1892 shortly before they began their aeronautical research and experimentation; the 1905 Wright Flyer III, at Carillon Historical Park (a fee is charged), 2001 S. Patterson Blvd.; the Huffman Prairie Flying Field, where they perfected their flyer (accessed from State Route 444); and the Paul Laurence Dunbar House State Memorial (a fee is charged), at 219 N. Paul Laurence Dunbar St. A museum is located in The Wright Cycle Company building at 22 South Williams. Partnership sites within the park include the Huffman Prairie Flying Field at Wright-Patterson Air Force Base; the Wright Flyer III in Carcllon Historical Park and the Dunbar House State Memorial. All are open to the public. A Dayton-area Aviation Trail driving tour of 45 sites associated with aviation history is described in a guidebook available at local bookstores.

Hopewell Culture National Historical Park

**16062 State Route 104
Chilliocothe, OH 45601
740-774-1125**

This 1,134-acre national historical park on the west bank of the Scioto River in south-central Ohio protects and interprets a major concentration of burial and ceremonial grounds of the Hopewell Culture, dating from at least 200 B.C. to around A.D. 500. Within one 13-acre area, a geometrically shaped enclosure formed by a three- to four-foot-high earthen wall, are 23 Indian burial mounds. The largest of these dome-shaped earthen structures are about 17 feet high and 90 feet in circumference. Archaeologists' discoveries there indicate that the Hopewell people achieved a remarkably high level of artistic development in their arts and crafts and used a wide variety of materials, which they obtained through an extensive intertribal trading network. Copper from the upper Great Lakes, for example, was made into ceremonial breastplates, headdresses, and ornaments in the shape of turtles, birds, and humans; quartz and mica from the Appalachian Mountains were made into ceremonial objects and weapons; and silver from Ontario was made into artistic burial objects. Other objects were fashioned from bone, shell, and obsidian—the latter possibly coming from the Yellowstone area of Wyoming.

The park's visitor center, which is open daily except Thanksgiving, Christmas, and New Year's Day, provides interpretive exhibits, including a fascinating presentation of Hopewell artifacts, along with an audiovisual program and publications. The park's visitor center is approximately four miles north of Chillicothe, on State Route 104.

James A. Garfield National Historic Site

**8095 Mentor Avenue
Mentor, OH 44060-5753
216-255-8722**

This seven-acre national historic site in northeast Ohio protects and interprets the property, called "Lawnfield," associated with the life of James A. Garfield, the 20th president of the United States. Garfield served in the presidency for only a few months in 1881, before being shot by an assassin and dying two months later. He had previously been a canal bargeman, carpenter, farmer, preacher, professor, college president, and an attorney at law. In 1859, he was elected to the Ohio state senate and served in the Union army during the Civil War, fighting in the battles of Shiloh and Chickamauga. The visitor center, located in the carriage house that dates from 1893, provides interpretive exhibits, audiovisual programs, and publications. The site, which is administered by the Western Reserve Historical Society, is open Tuesdays through Sundays, except national holidays such as Thanksgiving, Christmas, and New Year's Day. Access to the site from I-90 is at the Mentor-Kirtland/Route 306 exit, north two miles on State Route 306, and east two miles on Mentor Avenue (U.S. Route 20).

Perry's Victory and International Peace Memorial

**P.O. Box 549
Put-in Bay, OH 43456-0549
419-285-2184**

This 25-acre international peace memorial commemorates one of the most decisive naval battles of the War of 1812. In the battle, Commodore Oliver Hazard Perry led nine American vessels to victory over six British warships by capturing their entire fleet. This so-called Battle of Lake Erie helped persuade the British to cease their hostilities and enabled the United States to claim the Old Northwest. Since the end of the War of 1812 and the peacefully negotiated Treaty of Rush-Bagot in 1817, relations between the United States and Britain, and subsequently the United States and Canada, have been peaceful. Perry's victory is

93

honored with a 352-foot-tall, granite Doric column on South Bass Island. Visitors may ride an elevator from the second floor of the memorial to an open-air observation platform, 317 feet above Lake Erie. Access to the island is by passenger or automobile ferry from Catawba Point or by passenger ferry from Port Clinton from April through November.

William Howard Taft National Historic Site

2038 Auburn Avenue
Cincinnati, OH 45219-3025
513-684-3262

This three-acre national historic site protects and interprets the restored childhood home of William Howard Taft, the 27th president of the United States (1909-1913), and subsequently the tenth Chief Justice of the U.S. Supreme Court (1921-1930). He is the only person in U.S. history to hold both positions.

Taft was born in this two-story, Greek-revival-style brick house. Four rooms have been restored to their appearance during Taft's childhood, in the 1860s. Other rooms contain interpretive exhibits on Taft's life and accomplishments. The house is open daily for guided tours, except Thanksgiving, Christmas, and New Year's Day. Access to the site from I-71 northbound is at Exit 2 (stay in the right lane), then left at the first stoplight and up Dorchester Ave., right onto Auburn Ave., and a half-block to the site. From I-71 southbound, take Exit 3, then turn right onto William Howard Taft Rd., left onto Auburn Ave., and a half-mile to the site.

SOUTH DAKOTA

Jewel Cave National Monument

Rural Route 1, Box 60 AA
Custer, SD 57730-9608
605-673-2288

This 1,274-acre national monument, in the ponderosa pine-covered Black Hills of western South Dakota, protects this remarkable cave that contains sparkling calcite nailhead and dogtooth spar crystals ranging in color from

jewel-like shades of pink and purple to gray and bronze. Other fascinating formations include calcite stalactites, stalagmites, draperies, and columns; aragonite frostwork; intricate gypsum flowers, beards, spiders, and cotton; hydromagnesite balloons; and delicately branched, white helictites that resemble miniature, frosted bonsai trees. Visitors usually enter the 116-mile-long cave (the world's third longest) by elevator from the visitor center. A scenic tour, provided year-round, winds through a half-mile of electrically illuminated passageways. A candlelight tour, offered seasonally, begins at the cave's original entrance at a limestone outcrop in Hell Canyon. A tour for spelunkers, offered seasonally, provides a more challenging experience.

Of the nine species of bats that inhabit the monument, four, including the western big-eared bat, use the cave as a place to hibernate. Above ground, this area of the forested Black Hills includes many plants and animals. Mammals include mule deer, bobcat, coyote, porcupine, desert cottontail, thirteen-lined ground squirrel, and least chipmunk. Birds include red-tailed hawk, golden eagle, wild turkey, great horned owl, woodpeckers (Lewis's, red-headed, downy, and hairy), flicker, violet-green swallow, blue and pinyon jays, black-billed magpie, black-capped chickadee, white-breasted and red-breasted nuthatches, house and canyon wrens, ruby-crowned kinglet, western wood pewee, dusky flycatcher, mountain bluebirds, Townsend's solitaire, robin, warblers (yellow-rumped, MacGillivray's, orange-crowned, and yellowthroat), ovenbird, western tanager, black-headed grosbeak, rufous-sided towhee, chipping sparrow, dark-eyed junco, American goldfinch, red crossbill, and pine siskin. Flora includes ponderosa pine, plains cottonwood, quaking aspen, American elm, boxelder, mountain mahogany, chokecherry, snowberry, iris, pasqueflower, blue flax, blue bells, blue-eyed grass, scarlet gaura, larkspur, lupine, sego lilies, woolly verbena, evening primrose, shootingstar, dotted gayfeather, prairie groundsel, upright prairie and pale purple coneflowers, blanket flower, and black-eyed Susan.

The visitor center, open daily except Thanksgiving, Christmas, and New Year's Day,

provides interpretive exhibits, an audiovisual program, and publications. Cave tours are offered from May 1 through September. The National Park Service advises cave visitors to dress warmly and wear soft-soled, low-heeled shoes. Access to the monument is west 12 miles of Custer, South Dakota, on U.S. Route 16; or east 24 miles of Newcastle, Wyoming, on U.S. Route 16. Mount Rushmore National Memorial and Wind Cave National Park are also located in the Black Hills.

▲ *Jewel Cave National Monument historic entrance, South Dakota*

Mount Rushmore National Memorial

**P.O. Box 268
Keystone, SD 57751-0268
605-574-2523**

This 1,278-acre national memorial in the Black Hills of western South Dakota protects the colossal carved images of four U.S. presidents:

95

George Washington, Thomas Jefferson, Abraham Lincoln, and Theodore Roosevelt. From 1927 to 1941, sculptor Gutzon Borglum and his crew of assistants carved these 60-foot-high faces on the granite wall of Mount Rushmore. The heads were carved using an intricate system of measuring, known as "pointing," by which the measurements on a small model could be expanded twelve times and carefully calculated on the mountain's surface. In the *Saturday Evening Post* of January 1, 1947, former U.S. senator and South Dakota governor William J. Bulow was quoted as saying: "It takes a genius to figure out the proper perspective so that the carvings will look right from the point from which the human eye beholds them. Gutzon Borglum was that genius."

The national memorial has a visitor center, open daily except Christmas, that provides interpretive exhibits, audiovisual programs, and publications. The one-mile Presidential Trail loops through an area of ponderosa pines and a few scattered quaking aspens as it passes close to the base of the mountain. White mountain goats, a non-native species introduced into the area many years ago, are often seen along the trail. Near the visitor center, Mt. Rushmore Dining Room and Snack Bar, managed by AMFAC Parks and Resorts, offers cafeteria-style dining and a summertime short-order grill. Access to the memorial from I-90 at Rapid City, South Dakota, is southwest 24 miles on U.S. Route 16, and west just over a mile on State Route 244. Wind Cave National Park, Jewel Cave National Monument, and Custer State Park are also located in the Black Hills and Badlands National Park is to the east.

WISCONSIN

Ice Age National Scenic Trail

National Park Service
700 Rayovac Drive, Suite 100
Madison, WI 53711
608-264-5610

Extending 1,000 miles through Wisconsin, this national scenic trail meanders over geologically significant glacial moraines and links six of the nine parts of the Ice Age National Scientific Reserve (an area affiliated with the National Park System). The trail highlights a chain of moraine ridges that were created as continental glacial ice was melting, approximately 10,000 years ago. Roughly 500 miles of this trail are currently open to the public for hiking and cross-country skiing. Some stretches of the route are also popular for marathons and ski races.

Saint Croix National Scenic Riverway

P.O. Box 708
St. Croix Falls, WI 54024-0708
715-483-3284

This 92,735-acre national scenic riverway in northwest Wisconsin and adjacent Minnesota protects 252 miles of the St. Croix River and its tributary, the Namekagon. The northern part of the riverway is free-flowing and wild, as it winds through some of the most scenic and least developed country in the upper Midwest. There are wonderful opportunities for canoeing, boating, fishing, camping, seasonal guided boat tours, birdwatching, and other recreational activities. Facilities include canoe rentals, boat-launching sites, and campsites. A few short trails lead through the riverway, while longer hiking routes are available in adjacent state parks and forests. Public hunting is permitted in part of the riverway during the designated season. Access to the southern end of the upper part of the riverway is from U.S. Route 8 at St. Croix Falls, Wisconsin. U.S. Route 53 runs through much of Wisconsin's Namekagon River area. Access to the lower part of the riverway is on Wisconsin Route 35, which winds through the area between I-94 to the south and U.S. Route 8 to the north.

Friends of the Parks Organizations

Citizens Protecting Mount Rushmore
P.O. Box 706
Keystone, SD 57751
605-666-4913

Cuyahoga Valley Association
P.O. Box 222
Peninsula, OH 44264
216-657-2909

Fort Larned Old Guard, Inc.
Route 3
Larned, KS 67550
316-285-6911

Friends of Agate Fossil Beds, Inc.
P.O. Box 27
Gering, NE 69341
308-635-3161

Friends of Crystal River
(Sleeping Bear Dunes National Lakeshore)
P.O. Box 61
Glen Arbor, MI 49636
616-334-4708

Friends of Fort Union Trading Post
Bedford Route
Williston, ND 58801
701-572-9083

Friends of Grand Portage
506 W. Michigan
Duluth, MN 55802
218-772-8011

Friends of Indiana Dunes
c/o Indiana Dunes National Lakeshore
1100 N. Mineral Springs Drive
Porter, IN 46304
219-926-7561, ext. 230

Friends of Pictured Rocks
P.O. Box 10144
Lansing, MI 48901
517-371-6363

Friends of the Mississippi River
26 E. Exchange Street
St. Paul, MN 55101
612-222-2193

Friends of William Howard Taft Birthplace NHS
2058 Auburn Avenue
Cincinnati, OH 45219
513-684-3262

Ice Age Park and Trail Foundation
P.O. Box 422
Sheboygan, WI 53082

Jefferson National Expansion Historic Association
11 N. 4th Street
St. Louis, MO 63102
314-425-4468

Knife River Heritage Foundation
P.O. Box 284
Stanton, ND 58571
701-745-3250

Lewis and Clark Trail Heritage Foundation, Inc.
P.O. Box 3434
Great Falls, MT 59403

Mount Rushmore National Memorial Society
P.O. Box 1066
Rapid City, SD 57709
605-341-8883

Oregon-California Trails Association
P.O. Box 1019
Independence, MO 64051-0519
816-252-2276

Ozark Heritage Foundation
(Ozark National Scenic Riverway)
P.O. Box 490
Van Buren, MO 63965
314-323-4236

Ozark Riverkeepers Network
(Ozark National Scenic Riverway)
Star Route, Box 70C
Mountain View, MO 65548
417-256-6370

St. Croix River Association
P.O. Box 1032
Hudson, WI 54016

Santa Fe Trail Association
Route 3
Larned, KS 67550
316-285-2054

Voyageurs Region National Park Association
119 N. 4th Street
Minneapolis, MN 55401
612-333-5424

Wilson's Creek National Battlefield Foundation
P.O. Box 8163
Springfield, MO 65801
417-581-4387

Cooperating Associations

Badlands Natural History Association
Badlands National Park
P.O. Box 47
Interior, SD 57750
605-433-5489

Black Hills Parks and Forest Association
Route 1, Box 190-WCNP
Hot Springs, SD 57747
605-745-7020

Fort Union Trading Post Association
R.R. 3, Box 71
Williston, ND 58801
701-572-9083

George Washington Carver Birthplace Association
5646 Carver Road
Diamond, MO 64840
417-325-4151

Isle Royale Natural History Association
800 E. Lakeshore Drive
Houghton, MI 49931
906-482-7860

Jefferson National Expansion Historical Association
11 N. 4th Street
St. Louis, MO 63102
314-425-4472

Lake States Interpretive Association
3131 Highway 53
International Falls, MN 55649
218-283-2103

Mount Rushmore History Association
P.O. Box 444
Keystone, SD 57751
605-574-2523

National Park Trust
c/o Tallgrass Prairie National Preserve
P.O. Box 585
Cottonwood Falls, KS 66845
316-273-8139

National Trust for Historic Preservation
1785 Massachusetts Avenue, NW
Washington, DC 20036
202-673-4000

Oregon Trail Museum Association
c/o Scotts Bluff National Monument
P.O. Box 27
Gering, NE 69341
308-436-2975

Ozark National Riverways Historical Association
P.O. Box 490
Van Buren, MO 63965
573-323-4236

Pipestone Indian Shrine Association
c/o Pipestone National Monument
P.O. Box 27
Pipestone, MN 56164
507-825-5463

Southwest Parks and Monuments Association
211 N. Court Avenue
Tucson, AZ 85701
520-622-1999

Student Conservation Association
1800 N. Kent Street
Arlington, VA 22209
703-524-2441

**Theodore Roosevelt Nature and
History Association**
P.O. Box 167
Medora, ND 58645
701-623-4884

LOCAL COLOR

The Wildlife

"Texas" means friend.

Texas was a country before it was a state.

25 languages.

65 nationalities.

Texans believe life is too important to be dull.

The Wildflowers

The state flower is the Bluebonnet.

Over 5,000 species of wildflowers.

There's even a Wildflower Center (Thanks to Lady Bird Johnson).

Texas does not have blue grass. It just seems that way.

It's like a whole other country.®

Even the vacations are bigger in Texas. From the yarn-spinning charm of our native citizenry to hills carpeted with our native flowers, you'll find it all in Texas. It's more than you think. It's like a whole other country. For your free Texas travel guide, you can visit our web site at 💻 **www.TravelTex.com** or call us at ☎ **1-800-8888-TEX (Ext. 1290).** So give us a call, y'all.

NPCA Checks
Save Our Parks!

Every order helps preserve our country's most precious areas. Every time you order, royalties go directly to the National Parks and Conservation Association.

Return Address Labels - six scenes match your checks!

Hemp Checkbook Cover features the NPCA logo

Cotton Covers- select your favorite scene

Acadia

Everglades

Yellowstone

Arches

Smoky Mountains

Yosemite

utiful rotating ies features Great Smoky untains, Yosemite, hes, Yellowstone, dia, and Everglades ional Parks.

N A T I O N A L   P A R K S   C H E C K S   O R D E R   F O R M

ck Your Choice Below:	200 Singles	150 Duplicates	Total
National Parks Check Series (6 designs) (NP)	❑ $15.95	❑ $17.95	$_____
240 National Parks Labels (6 designs) (NP-LB) ....Add $12.95			$_____

ckbook Covers:

Hemp Logo Cover (HNP-UQLO)..Add $14.95		$_____
Cotton Cover (CNP -UQLO)..Add $11.95		$_____

Select Scene: ❑ Acadia ❑ Everglades ❑ Yellowstone
❑ Arches ❑ Smoky Mountains ❑ Yosemite

SUBTOTAL $_____

Add 6.5% tax *for Minnesota residents only* $_____

Delivery ❑ $1.95 per item *OR* PRIORITY ❑ $3.95 per item $_____

TOTAL ENCLOSED: $_____
GD

yment type

❑ *Check enclosed–make payable to:* Message!Products™ *No COD's*

❑ *Debit my checking account (CHECK ORDERS ONLY)* Signature_____

❑ *Charge to:* ❑ *Visa* ❑ *Mastercard* ❑ *American Express* ❑ *Discover*

No._____Exp. Date____/____ Signature_____

IMPORTANT! Include the following with this form:

❑ Voided check indicating a starting number # _____ for your new order
(If none given we will start your order at 101)

❑ Deposit ticket from the same account

❑ Three lines of personalization for matching labels: *(see left side!)*

_____

_____

_____

❑ Daytime Telephone Number:(_____)
(CONFIDENTIAL - in case of questions about your order only)

Please allow 3-5 weeks processing & delivery OR 1-3 weeks for PRIORITY delivery

To order, send complete form to:

Message!Products	*or fax to:*
P.O. Box 64800	1-800-790-6684
St. Paul, MN	*or order online!*
55164-0800	www.messagecheck.com

QUESTIONS? 1-800-243-2565